Also by James W. Loewen

The Mississippi Chinese: Between Black and White

Mississippi: Conflict and Change (with Charles Sallis et al.)

Social Science in the Courtroom

Lies My Teacher Told Me: Everything Your American History Textbook Got Wrong

Lies Across America: What Our Historic Sites Get Wrong

Sundown Towns: A Hidden Dimension of American Racism

Teaching What Really Happened

The Confederate and Neo-Confederate Reader

Lies My Teacher Told Me About Christopher Columbus

What Your History Books Got Wrong

Second Edition

JAMES W. LOEWEN

THE NEW PRESS

NEW YORK
LONDON

Requests for permission to reproduce selections from this book should be mailed to: Permissions
Department, The New Press, 120 Wall Street, 31st floor, New York, NY 10005.

Originally published as *The Truth About Columbus: A Subversively True Poster Book for a Dubiously
Celebratory Occasion* by The New Press, New York, 1992
This revised and updated edition published by The New Press, New York, 2014
Distributed by Perseus Distribution

CIP data available
ISBN 978-1-59558-985-9 (pbk/poster)

The New Press publishes books that promote and enrich public discussion and understanding
of the issues vital to our democracy and to a more equitable world. These books are made possible by the
enthusiasm of our readers; the support of a committed group of donors, large and small; the collaboration
of our many partners in the independent media and the not-for-profit sector; booksellers, who often
hand-sell New Press books; librarians; and above all by our authors.

www.thenewpress.com

Book design and composition by Bookbright Media
This book was set in Adobe Caslon Pro and News Gothic

Printed in the United States of America

2 4 6 8 10 9 7 5 3 1

Contents

An examination of the way the following textbooks tell the story of Christopher Columbus:

Joyce Appleby, Alan Brinkley, and James M. McPherson
The American Journey (2000)

Thomas A. Bailey and David M. Kennedy
The American Pageant (1983)

David M. Kennedy, Lizabeth Cohen, and Thomas A. Bailey
The American Pageant (2006)

Nancy Bauer
The American Way (1979)

Carol Berkin and Leonard Wood
Land of Promise (1983)

Daniel J. Boorstin and Brooks Mather Kelley
A History of the United States (1989)

Daniel J. Boorstin and Brooks Mather Kelley
A History of the United States (2005)

Paul Boyer
Holt American Nation (2003)

Andrew Cayton, Elisabeth Israels Perry, Linda Reed, and Allan M. Winkler
America: Pathways to the Present (2005)

Gerald A. Danzer, J. Jorge Klor de Alva, Larry S. Krieger,
Louis E. Wilson, and Nancy Woloch
The Americans (2007)

James West Davidson and Mark H. Lytle
The United States—A History of the Republic (1981)

Robert A. Divine, T. H. Breen, George M. Fredrickson, and R. Hal Williams
America Past and Present (1987)

John A. Garraty with Aaron Singer and Michael Gallagher
American History (1982)

Robert Green, Laura L. Becker, and Robert E. Coviello
The American Tradition (1984)

Allan O. Kownslar and Donald B. Frizzle
Discovering American History (1974)

Gary B. Nash, Julie Roy Jeffrey, John R. Howe, Peter J. Frederick,
Allen F. Davis, and Allan M. Winkler
The American People (1990)

Ira Peck, Steven Jantzen, and Daniel Rosen
American Adventures (1987)

Philip Roden, Robynn Greer, Bruce Kraig, and Betty Bivins
Life and Liberty (1984)

Robert Sobel, Roger LaRaus, Linda Ann De Leon, and Harry P. Morris
The Challenge of Freedom (1982)

Social Science Staff of the Educational Research Council of America
The American Adventure (1975)

Paul Lewis Todd and Merle Curti
Rise of the American Nation (1982)

Paul Lewis Todd and Merle Curti
Triumph of the American Nation (1990)

INTRODUCTION

In fourteen hundred and ninety-two, Christopher Columbus sailed in from the blue. U.S. history textbooks portray him as our first great hero. So does our whole culture. Indeed, now that Presidents' Day has combined Washington's and Lincoln's birthdays, Columbus is one of only two people the United States honors by name in a national holiday. (The other is Martin Luther King Jr.) The one date from history class that everyone remembers is 1492.

I have surveyed 22 widely used high school and middle school textbooks of U.S. history to learn what they say about Christopher Columbus.[1] I have also asked hundreds of my college students to tell me what they remember from high school and middle school about Columbus and the European exploration of the Americas. And I have given workshops for K–12 history and social studies teachers across the country on how to teach about Columbus, in the process exploring how they *do* teach about him. So I have a good idea what gets taught and learned about Columbus in many schools in the United States.

Columbus was so pivotal that historians use him, like Jesus, to divide history; the Americas before 1492 are called "pre-Columbian." The textbooks give Columbus a lot of space —a thousand words on average, a map, a portrait, and an illustration (of a ship or a landing). They make quite a story out of his life. Their heroic collective account goes something like this:

> Born in Genoa, Italy, of humble parents, Christopher Columbus grew up to become an experienced seafarer. He sailed the Atlantic as far as Iceland and West Africa. His experiences convinced him that the world must be round. Therefore the fabled riches of the East—spices, silk, and gold—could be had, he reasoned, by sailing west, replacing the overland route through the Middle East, which the Turks had closed off to commerce. To fund his enterprise, he beseeched monarch after monarch in western Europe. Finally, after being dismissed once more by Ferdinand and Isabella of Spain, Columbus got his chance. Queen Isabella decided to underwrite a modest expedition. He outfitted three pitifully small ships, *Niña*, *Pinta*, and *Santa María*, and set forth from Spain. After a difficult westward journey of more than two months, during which his mutinous crew threatened to throw him overboard, he discovered the West Indies on October 12, 1492. Unfortunately, although he made three more voyages to America, Columbus never knew he had discovered a New World. He died in obscurity, unappreciated and penniless. Without his daring, though, American history would have been very different—for in a sense he made it all possible.

Unfortunately, almost everything in this traditional account is either wrong or unknowable. The textbooks have taken us on a trip of their own, away from the facts of history, into the realm of myth. Moreover, the

---

Doing History: What Do *You* Know About Christopher Columbus?

Answer these questions off the top of your head. Record your replies in a safe place (the inside back cover, if this is your book). Where was Columbus born? What did he do in 1492 (with as many details as you can recall)? in 1493 (with details)? Rank him on a scale of −3 (cruel) to +3 (kind). He died −3 (poor) to +3 (rich). Write a paragraph about his most important impact on history.

---

1. The 22 textbooks are: Joyce Appleby, Alan Brinkley, and James McPherson, *The American Journey* (NY: Glencoe McGraw-Hill, 2000); Thomas A. Bailey and David M. Kennedy, *The American Pageant* (Lexington, MA: D.C. Heath, 1983); David M. Kennedy, Lizabeth Cohen, and Thomas A. Bailey, *The American Pageant* (Boston: Houghton Mifflin, 2006); Nancy Bauer, *The American Way* (New York: Holt, Rinehart & Winston, 1979); Carol Berkin and Leonard Wood, *Land of Promise* (Glenview, IL: Scott, Foresman, 1983); Daniel J. Boorstin and Brooks Mather Kelley, *A History of the United States* (Needham, MA: Prentice Hall, 1989); ibid. (2005); Andrew Cayton et al., *America: Pathways to the Present* (Upper Saddle River, NJ: Pearson Prentice-Hall, 2005); Gerald A. Danzer et al., *The Americans* (Evanston, IL: McDougal Littell, 2007); James West Davidson and Mark H. Lytle, *The United States—A History of the Republic* (Englewood Cliffs, NJ: Prentice-Hall, 1981); Robert A. Divine et al., *America Past and Present* (Glenview, IL: Scott, Foresman, 1987); John A. Garraty with Aaron Singer and Michael Gallagher, *American History* (New York: Harcourt Brace Jovanovich, 1982); Robert Green, Laura L. Becker, and Robert E. Coviello, *The American Tradition* (Columbus, OH: Charles E. Merrill, 1984); Allan O. Kownslar and Donald B. Frizzle, *Discovering American History* (New York: Holt, Rinehart & Winston, 1974); Gary B. Nash et al., *The American People* (New York: Harper & Row, 1990); Ira Peck, Steven Jantzen, and Daniel Rosen, *American Adventures* (Austin, TX: Steck-Vaughn, 1987); Philip Roden et al., *Life and Liberty* (Glenview, IL: Scott, Foresman, 1984); Robert Sobel et al., *The Challenge of Freedom* (River Forest, IL: Laidlaw Brothers, 1982); Social Science Staff of the Educational Research Council of America, *The American Adventure* (Boston: Allyn & Bacon, 1975); Paul Lewis Todd and Merle Curti, *Rise of the American Nation* (Orlando: Harcourt Brace Jovanovich, 1982); Paul Lewis Todd and Merle Curti, *Triumph of the American Nation* (Orlando: Harcourt Brace Jovanovich, 1990); and Paul Boyer, *Holt American Nation* (Austin, TX: Holt, Rinehart & Winston, 2003).

textbooks leave out just about everything important that we *do* know about Columbus and the European exploration of the Americas. They omit the causes, most of what Columbus actually did, and some of the results of his voyages. In place of these, to make him a bigger hero, they invent all kinds of details that never happened.

Reading this book and the accompanying poster will be something of a voyage of exploration itself. We shall enter a world unknown to those who read only conventional history textbooks—the world of historic evidence. We will see what historians really know about Columbus, based on the original sources, and compare it to what the textbooks tell us about the man and his mission. Textbooks offer a journey into never-never land, where authors make up what they want us to believe about Columbus instead of revealing what really happened. Amnesia seems to afflict our textbooks: a hundred years ago we knew important historical facts that now we seem to have forgotten. Finally, we shall see that the true significance of Columbus's four voyages to the Americas was not that he "discovered" them—which he did not—but what he did with them. In the process, we will discover how history is made, how it is distorted, and how it sometimes becomes more accurate.

Just as the world was never the same after Columbus's voyages, if this book succeeds, your world will not be quite the same. You will see how different biases can affect the writing of history, even of basic textbooks. Knowing how they lied to you about Columbus, you may be more critical of what they tell you about other topics.

SOMEBODY WAS ALREADY LIVING HERE

Every textbook tells that people lived in the Americas before Christopher Columbus landed. However, when authors swing into what they see as their main story—the settlement of the Americas by Europeans—Native Americans[2] pretty much drop out of some books. The omissions begin with their presentations of Columbus. American Indians play bit parts in the Columbus story textbooks tell. The 2005 edition[3] of *A History of the United States*, by Daniel Boorstin, former Librarian of Congress, and Brooks Mather Kelley, former chief archivist at Yale

University, devotes almost two thousand words to the story of Columbus's four voyages to America. This is the longest account in any of the 22 books I surveyed. Yet in this account, Native Americans get only five words: "The natives called it Guanahani, and Columbus named it San Salvador."

Boorstin and Kelley do go on to allot their next two pages of text, one page of photos, and a map to American Indians. This small section of 1,250 words tries to cover 40,000 years and more than 400 societies, from Peru to the Arctic, in less space than Columbus gets!

Several books do much better. Five books devote their first chapter to Native Americans. *The American Adventure* gives three chapters—40 pages—to "The Earliest Immigrants." Nine books, including five of the six newest, also supply interesting information on Native Americans in the twentieth century. They show that the issues that Columbus raised are not yet settled.

Textbooks Underestimate the Population of the Americas

What should U.S. history textbooks tell us about the people who lived here when Columbus came calling? First, we need to know how many lived here. Calculating population sounds boring. It's not. Estimates of Ameri-

This Catlin painting of members of the Mandan tribe in North Dakota dramatizes the Native American population decline. In 1838, within eight years of his finishing it, smallpox struck the Mandans and reduced their number from 1,600 to just 31. That's why Catlin titled it *The Last Race*.

---

2. A later section discusses whether the first Americans should be called Indians or Native Americans.
3. This edition was still for sale as of late 2013. Henceforth, I shall include year of publication only when the edition cited is *not* the most recent.

can Indian population have gone through an interesting cycle. In 1840 George Catlin, a painter and student of American Indian culture, estimated that in 1492 fourteen million American Indians lived in what became the United States and Canada. He believed two million were still alive in the 1830s, when he was painting portraits of surviving American Indians in the West. But by 1921, anthropologist James Mooney would conclude that only one million Native Americans lived in what is now the United States in 1492.

Beginning in 1947, scholars have returned to estimates of four to twenty million. They have carefully assembled reports from the very first European visitors, before disease and increased warfare struck down so many Natives. In 1975, Francis Jennings took some pains to demolish the Mooney figure. He showed the incorrect assumptions it rested upon and concluded that ten to twenty million was more accurate.[4]

How do the 22 textbooks I surveyed, all written after Jennings, treat this topic? Not very well. Here textbooks reach a controversy. Authors might let readers in on this furious debate of the 1960s and early 1970s. They might tell how and why the estimates changed. Most don't. They seem to feel they must present "facts" for students to "learn." Therefore they hide the debate. Instead, most simply state numbers—very different numbers! *The Challenge of Freedom* believes "nearly one million Indians lived in North America." Since most of these surely lived in Mexico, that spares only a couple hundred thousand for the United States and Canada. *American History* suggests that one million people lived in the United States and Canada. Boorstin and Kelley say four million. *American Adventures* proposes "as many as ten million." The most common answer, supplied by five books, is the old discredited one million figure. Authors of several books, like *The Challenge of Freedom*, do not seem to know that Mexico is part of North America![5] Seven books omit the subject of Native population altogether. Several of the most recent textbooks make no estimate at all. This prevents them from being wrong, but surely a better solution would be to let students know that there is an issue here.

Authors Seem Obliged to Give Answers Rather Than Teach Issues

It's pretty funny to realize that students in some classes are learning fewer than a million, while those in other classes learn more than ten million. This shows that you can't just memorize answers from a textbook, not even about something as "factual" as population numbers.

Doing History: When Was Your Town First Settled?

Native Americans first settled many towns and cities in what is now the United States. European and African newcomers then either lived among the Natives or moved in after they died. Early British colonists used former American Indian cornfields, avoiding the work of clearing the trees and rocks. That's why so many town names in the East—Marshfield, Springfield, Deerfield—end in "field." Across America, historical markers reserve "settle" and "settlers" for Europeans. A stone marker in the center of Greenfield, Massachusetts, announces:

Town of Greenfield
Settled 1686
Incorporated 1753.

This is bad history. Pocumtuck Indians cleared Greenfield's green fields millennia ago. In 1637, 50 years before 1686, Greenfield Natives sent 50 canoes full of corn, amounting to 500 bushels, to help the starving British settlers of Massachusetts. Then disease and a Mohawk attack killed the Pocumtucks. Signs like Greenfield's reinforce the old "virgin wilderness" myth. The American landscape would have a very different feel if all such markers read:

Town of Greenfield
Settled c. 5000 B.P.
Resettled by Europeans 1686.

Was your town settled by American Indians before outsiders arrived? Does a marker acknowledge their settlement? Should it?

4. Only one of my 22 textbooks includes reference footnotes. Publishers claim that footnotes would be too hard for students. It's really just the opposite. Having no footnotes is hard for students, because it makes it difficult to see if authors got their facts right. For a review of the population literature, see Melissa Meyer and Russell Thornton, "Indians and the Numbers Game," in *New Directions in American Indian History*, ed. Colin Calloway (Norman: U. of Oklahoma Press, 1988). See also Francis Jennings, *The Invasion of America: Indians, Colonialism, and the Cant of Conquest* (Chapel Hill: U. of North Carolina Press, 1975), 16.
5. One of the most controversial topics of the 1990s was the North America Free Trade Agreement, controversial precisely because U.S. workers feared that Mexico's much lower wages would draw many manufacturing plants south of the border. All of the people listed as authors of even the newest textbooks were adults in 1994, when NAFTA went into effect. Yet *The Americans*, for example, says only five million lived in North America. Mexico's population when the Spanish arrived was at least twenty million.

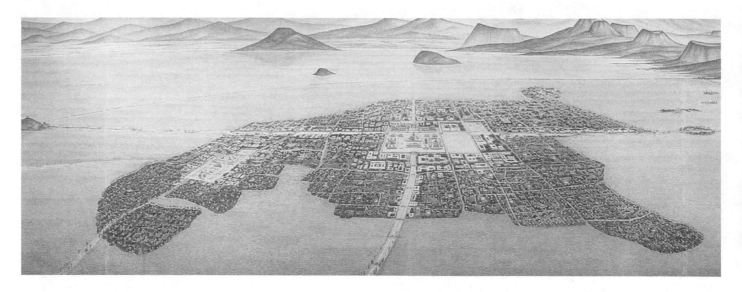

Tenochtitlan (now Mexico City) was a metropolis of 100,000 to 300,000 people.[6] When Cortés first saw it, he proclaimed it "larger and more pleasant than any city in Europe." This is the central market as shown in the "Seeds of Change" exhibition at the Smithsonian Institution.

Nevertheless, the problem isn't with the estimates—it is with the approach. Why do authors feel they must give simple answers like these? Population estimates aren't something to memorize. They are based on reasoning, arguments, and weighing of evidence. Only two books admit there is a controversy, and both do so only in footnotes. In its footnote, *The American Pageant* says, "Much controversy surrounds estimates of the pre-Columbian Native American population." Unfortunately, *Pageant* then goes on to give two wildly different specific estimates: 54,000,000 for North and South America combined, on page 6, followed by "no more than 4,000,000" for North America on page 10.[7] Even though their larger figure is in line with current scholarship, whoever wrote page 10 must not have read page 6, because page 10 tells how Natives "were so few in number" and "so thinly spread" that just a few people "padded through the whispering, primeval forests and paddled across the sparkling, virgin waters of North America." At least *Pageant* mentions the controversy, however. All other textbooks but one keep students unaware of it.

Terms like "virgin wilderness" are rarely appropriate. Columbus himself wrote that the Americas were "filled with innumerable people." When he landed on Haiti, he saw towns and fields without end. Columbus made Haiti his headquarters and called it Hispaniola—Little Spain. (Hispaniola is now divided into two independent nations, Haiti and the Dominican Republic.) In 1496 Columbus asked his brother, Bartholomew, to oversee a census of the Arawaks on Haiti. Bartholomew's men counted 1,130,000, excluding children under fourteen and very old people. At that time the Spaniards controlled about half the island, so its total population was probably more than twice that number.

Bartolomé de Las Casas spent most of his long life in the Caribbean, working for better treatment of the Natives and writing a history of Spanish-Indian relations. He included summaries of the journals that Columbus kept of his first and third voyages. Since Columbus's original journals are lost, Las Casas's summaries are the best record we have of these crucial undertakings. Las Casas estimated that Haiti "contained more than three or four million people" when Columbus landed. Modern researchers agree.[8]

What about the rest of the Western Hemisphere? Current scholarship suggests that in 1492 between 50 million and 90 million people lived in the Americas, including 5 to 20 million in what is now the United States and Can-

6. Robert F. Spencer and Jesse D. Jennings, *The Native Americans* [New York: Harper and Row, 1977], 480.
7. *Pageant* is another book whose authors do not know that Mexico is in North America.
8. The most detailed analysis of Haitian population in 1492 is Sherburne Cook and Woodrow Borah, *Essays in Population History: Mexico and the Caribbean* (Berkeley: U. of California Press, 1971), 1:376–410. See also Alfred W. Crosby Jr., *The Columbian Exchange* (Westport, CT: Greenwood, 1972), 45; Benjamin Keen, "Black Legend," in *The Christopher Columbus Encyclopedia* (New York: Simon and Schuster, 1991); Las Casas, *The Tears of the Indians* (Stanford, CA: Academic Reprints, n.d. [1656]), 3; and Kirkpatrick Sale, *The Conquest of Paradise* (New York: Knopf, 1990), 160–61.

ada. About 25 million lived in Mexico alone.[9] (By way of contrast, about 5 to 8 million people lived in Spain, 5 million in England, Scotland, and Wales, and 75 to 90 million in all of Europe.)[10]

TEACHING AGAINST THE CULTURE

Already we see that U.S. history courses do not operate in a vacuum. Our popular culture does not say very much about plane geometry, photosynthesis, or Shakespeare's sonnets, but it says a lot about Christopher Columbus and American Indians. For example, here is a Mother's

The cartoonist buys the false myth that Christopher Columbus showed that the earth was round.

Day cartoon playing on the "fact" that before Columbus people thought that the earth was flat.

Most people believe the culture that surrounds them, so it's hard to break out of it. Teachers and textbooks have to make a point of challenging the culture when it says something bogus. Once they learn better, students need

---

9. These Native American population estimates are based on eight sources: P.M. Ashburn, *The Ranks of Death* (New York: Coward-McCann, 1947); Cook and Borah, *Essays in Population History*, vol. 1; Crosby, *The Columbian Exchange*; Henry F. Dobyns, *Their Number Become Thinned* (Knoxville: U. of Tennessee Press, 1983), 42; Jennings, *The Invasion of America*, 16–30; William H. McNeill, *Plagues and Peoples* (Garden City, NY: Anchor, 1976); Howard Simpson, *Invisible Armies* (Indianapolis: Bobbs-Merrill, 1980); and Russell Thornton, *American Indian Holocaust and Survival: A Population History Since 1492* (Norman: U. of Oklahoma Press, 1987).
10. European population estimates are based on Crosby, *The Columbian Exchange*, and William L. Langer, "The Black Death," *Scientific American*, February 1964.

to teach more accurate information to their friends and parents.

Were American Indians Primitive or Civilized?

Our history books not only imply that few people lived here, they also picture most of those who did as primitive. *American Adventures* describes Columbus's arrival this way: "Who were these people who greeted them on the shore? They were practically naked. They were not dressed in fancy silk robes and jewelry." *Adventures* is right that the Natives were practically naked. Today many Europeans in Haiti are also practically naked Club Med vacationers. It's a warm country. Being naked doesn't mean one lacks sophistication or culture.

Some recent textbooks maintain this "primitive" stereotype. Boorstin and Kelley, for example, put down all Native Americans because they "never invented the wheel," "had no iron tools," "had not built ships to cross the ocean," and generally "ceased to progress." "North of Mexico," in particular, "most of the people lived in wandering tribes and led a simple life." They were "mainly hunters and gatherers of wild food. An exceptional few—in Arizona and New Mexico—settled in one place and became farmers." Actually, we shall see that most Natives in what is now the United States farmed, until Europeans forced many of them to become nomadic.

American History by John Garraty indulges in the most open use of the primitive-to-civilized division. "With historical imagination it is not hard to see the Spanish conquerors as the first Americans must have seen them. Here were gods come from heaven to rule them," Garraty writes. "These gods looked down at frail canoes from enormous floating fortresses. How strong they seemed in their shining clothing, how rich in color."

The Wreck of *Santa María*

Garraty did not need to resort to "historical imagination." Primary sources, from people who were on the scene, are the basic evidence for history. *American History* could have used Columbus's own journal to tell the true story of the "floating fortress" *Santa María*. On Christmas Day, 1492, Columbus's flagship hit rocks off Haiti. Columbus immediately told the nearest leader, Guacanagarí. In Columbus's account, summarized by

Las Casas, Guacanagarí "wept and sent all his people from the town, with many large canoes to unload the ship. This was done and everything was taken from the decks in a very short space of time. So great was the haste and diligence which that king showed!" The next day Guacanagarí told Columbus "that he had given to the Christians who were on shore two very large houses, and that he would give them more if it were necessary, and as many canoes as they needed to load and unload the ship." Las Casas goes on to quote Columbus's own words: "'They are so loyal,' says the admiral, 'and without greed for what is not theirs, and so above all the others was that virtuous king.'"

Thus, right from the start, American Indians saw that the Europeans were not gods, but could suffer setbacks like any men. Right from the start, the Natives knew that their own canoes were not so frail but could help rescue supplies from "the enormous floating fortresses." I know no evidence from primary sources that the Arawaks thought the Spaniards "were gods come from heaven to rule them." Quite the contrary: after *Santa María* wrecked, Columbus left some 40 men on Haiti in a fort built from its remains. When he returned on his second voyage, he found them all dead. They had raped and plundered the Natives until the Arawaks killed them. Right from the start, then, Garraty gives a false picture of European superiority and Native primitiveness. Garraty is not alone. Not one book tells how American Indians saved the wreckage of *Santa María*. Only one gives us the name of Guacanagarí or any other Native Columbus ever met. *Journey* does provide a scene from a novel by Michael Dorris, a Native American writer, told from the viewpoint of an Arawak girl who encounters Columbus. No other book gives us anything from a Native viewpoint.[11]

Primitive or Civilized—A False Dichotomy

Native Americans have been rebuking textbook writers for their selective use of the term "civilized" for a long time. In 1927, an organization called the Grand Council Fire of American Indians called school histories "unjust to the life of our people." They went on to question, "What is civilization? Its marks are a noble religion and philosophy, original arts, stirring music, rich story and legend. We had these. Then we were not savages, but a civilized race."[12]

11. *The Americans* provides a little box, "Interact with History," that purports to get students to take a Native viewpoint. "You live on a Caribbean island. . . . Your society hunts game freely. . . . Now you sense that your world is about to change: the ships you see approaching are like nothing you have encountered before. How will the arrival of a strange people change your way of life?" Surely written by someone who never read anything from an Arawak viewpoint, language like this merely invites armchair theorizing, not historical research.
12. Quoted in Rupert Costo and Jeanette Henry, *Textbooks and the American Indian* (San Francisco: Indian Historical Press, 1970).

Five hundred years ago, Bartolomé de Las Casas knew better than to call the Arawaks and Caribs noncivilized. "They used their leisure in honest recreation, such as strenuous ball games, dances, and songs that recited their historic past," he wrote. "They also made very beautiful objects with their hands when they were not occupied with agricultural, fishing, or domestic chores." This illustration shows the Caribs at home on St. Vincent, before Europeans destroyed their lifestyle. Agostino Brunias painted it in the West Indies in 1790.

Some U.S. history textbooks do recognize the diversity of Native American cultures. These books don't label all Native societies "primitive," exempting Incas, Mayas, and Aztecs. Still, when they admire those hierarchical American Indian societies that were more like our society today, authors reinforce ethnocentrism. Ethnocentrism means thinking of one's own culture as better than anyone else's. Boorstin and Kelley, for instance, say, "The great empires of old America—of the Mayas, the Incas, and the Aztecs—were all in Mexico or south. North of Mexico most of the people lived in wandering tribes and led a simple life. North American Indians were mainly hunters and gatherers of wild food."

This won't do. First, it's wrong: most American Indians were farmers. More important, ranking societies on a scale from primitive ("simple," in the words of Boorstin and Kelley) to civilized doesn't work. Was Nazi Germany civilized, for instance? Most sociologists, referring to Germany's advanced technology, would answer yes. Does that mean we prefer the "civilized" Third Reich to the "primitive" Arawaks who met Columbus? *The Amer-*

ican Adventure implies that we do: "Unlike the simple noncivilized peoples of the Caribbean, the Aztec were rich and prosperous." In everyday conversation, on the other hand, "civilized" means polite and refined, the opposite of savage. Using this definition, we must consider the Arawaks civilized, while Columbus and his Spaniards, as we shall see, must be deemed primitive, even savage—like the Nazis and the bloodthirsty Aztecs.

Unlike some textbook authors, Columbus knew that Native Americans were not primitive. On his fourth voyage, off Bonacca Island in the Caribbean, he encountered a Mayan trading canoe so big that it required 25 paddlers. It was "freighted with merchandise" and had "a palm leaf awning like that which the Venetian gondolas carry," in the words of his son Ferdinand. "This gave complete protection against the rain and waves. Under this awning were the children and women and all the baggage and merchandise." This arrangement for maritime transport was technologically advanced enough to merit some discussion in Columbus's journal.

Way back in 1931, writer Gregory Mason lambasted textbooks for treating Native Americans as primitives. He used Columbus's encounter with this canoe as an example. "Let us keep the picture of that maritime merchant in our minds," wrote Mason, "for it induces a more accurate conception of pre-Columbian America than we can get from any historical textbook in our schools."[13] Sadly, even today no book mentions this incident. Even worse, despite good intentions, despite giving more space to pre-Columbian Native cultures than they used to, textbooks still contrast primitive Indians and modern Europeans.

This comparison is inaccurate. American Indian societies varied before 1492 just as much as societies in Eurasia and Africa. The Incas of Peru and Ecuador organized themselves into a large nation-state. Under Ferdinand and Isabella, Spain had only just become such a state. The Algonquians in New England were organized by towns, which in turn loosely confederated into tribes. So were most people in eastern Europe. Natives on the Great Plains were organized as family clans, as were people in Scotland. Thus, we cannot lump American Indians together as primitive, Europeans as civilized, even regarding form of government.

"Tribe" is also a problem word. When Serbs and Croats battled in former Yugoslavia, we didn't call them tribes. When Catholics and Protestants fought in Northern Ireland, we didn't call that tribal warfare. We seem to

13. *Columbus Came Late* (New York: Century, 1931), 197–98.

reserve "tribe" for groupings among Africans and Native Americans. Some Native Americans don't mind "tribe," believing "nation" is an inappropriate European concept. Others prefer to use "nation," because they don't like how our textbooks contrast "civilized" European nations and "primitive" American tribes.

THE WORDS WE USE INFLUENCE HOW WE THINK

In 1973, Adam Nordwall, also known as Fortunate Eagle, an Ojibwa Indian, flew with his Shoshone wife to Rome, planted a banner, and "discovered" Italy. Then he requested, "take me to your leader!" This photo shows Nordwall with the Pope shortly afterward.

Words such as "primitive," "civilized," and "tribe" affect how we think and act. "Discover" is another problem word. You'll notice this book usually substitutes "reached" or "encountered." "Discover" usually means "finding something previously unknown to humans." Thus, Marie Curie discovered radium in 1898. But textbooks use "discover" to mean "finding something previously unknown to *whites*." That's just how Columbus himself used the word when he wrote in a letter to a Spanish nobleman, "I discovered very many islands, *filled with innumerable people,* all of which I took possession of."

"Discovering" the Known

Notice the words I italicized: how can one person "discover" what another already knows and owns?

In reality, Columbus did *not* discover a new world. When he ceremoniously "took possession of the land in the name of the Catholic Sovereigns," as his son Ferdinand put it, "many Indians assembled to watch." People had discovered "the land" 12,000 to 70,000 years earlier. Nonetheless, textbooks to this day use "discover."

"Discover" is no minor matter. In Columbus's will, he maintained his view that the West Indies were his because he had "found" them: "I presented [to Spain] the

Indies. . . . I gave them, as a thing that was mine." The United States has used the same rule about American Indian land. In 1823, Chief Justice John Marshall of the U.S. Supreme Court decreed that Cherokees had some rights to their land in Georgia because they "occupied" it. However, whites had superior rights because they "discovered" it. How the Cherokees managed to occupy Georgia without previously discovering it, he neglected to explain.[14]

After "discovering" an island and meeting a tribe of Americans new to them, the Spaniards read aloud to them in Spanish what came to be called "the Requirement." Here is one version:

> I implore you to recognize the Church as a lady
> and in the name of the Pope take the King as lord
> of this land and obey his mandates. If you do not
> do it, I tell you that with the help of God I will
> enter powerfully against you all. I will make war
> everywhere and every way that I can. I will subject
> you to the yoke and obedience to the church and
> to his majesty. I will take your women and children
> and make them slaves. . . . The deaths and injuries
> that you will receive from here on will be your own
> fault and not that of his majesty nor of the gentle-
> men that accompany me.[15]

You can imagine what happened next. The Natives, who had never heard Spanish before, had no idea what the Spaniards had just said to them. The Spaniards, having satisfied their consciences by "giving the Indians a chance" to convert to Christianity, were now free to do

---

Doing History: "Discovery" Markers

Locate a "discovered" marker near you. Research it. Did Native Americans really discover the feature first?

---

14. See *Johnson v. M'Intosh*, discussed in Robert K. Faulkner, *The Jurisprudence of John Marshall* (Princeton, NJ: Princeton U. Press, 1968), 53.
15. The Requirement has been widely reprinted. This translation is from "500 Years of Indigenous and Popular Resistance Campaign," Guatemala Committee for Peasant Unity, 1990.

whatever they wanted with the people they had just "discovered."

Every single textbook uses "discover" to describe what Columbus did. Interestingly, they never say Marco Polo "discovered" China, not even in quotation marks. Authors are struggling with this issue. Some know "discover" is biased language. *Land of Promise* uses it: "If Columbus had not discovered the New World, others soon would have." Three sentences later, the authors try to take it back: "As is often pointed out, Columbus did not really 'discover' America. When he arrived on this side of the Atlantic there were perhaps 20 or more million people already here." Taking back the specific word is not enough, however: *Land of Promise*'s whole approach is of whites discovering primitives who didn't really know where they were, rather than two groups meeting in a mutual encounter. Thus, *Land of Promise* titles its first chapter "The Old World Finds the New." That's a good example of ethnocentrism. Several recent textbooks do treat 1492 as a meeting of three cultural areas (Africa was soon involved) rather than a discovery by one. All textbooks should abandon "discover."

Not a "New World," Not an Age of Exploration

"New World" is another biased term. The bias is Eurocentrism, which means to make Europe the center of all things. Eurocentrism imposes a false, one-sided perspective on history. People had lived in the Americas for thousands of years. The Americas were not new to American Indians in 1492. Europe was. At the end of 1492, Columbus kidnapped and took across the Atlantic half a dozen Arawaks. To them Spain was just as unexpected, just as interesting—and just as "new"—as Haiti was to Columbus. For "New World," authors should substitute "The Americas" or "Western Hemisphere."

Life and Liberty knows to avoid "New World": "When Christopher Columbus led his fleet of three ships to the Americas in 1492, a new chapter in world history began." But *Life and Liberty* goes on to commit a euphemism—a term milder and less accurate than the word it replaces.

> The next 200 years were part of a great age of *exploration*. People from Europe traveled to all parts of the world. They met people and explored lands their parents had not known existed. They also began European settlements, or colonies, in many places, including the Americas.

Doing History: Other Eurocentric Terms

After Columbus, Europe became the point of reference for our terms for much of the world. Americans usually write "Near East" for Iraq, Jordan, Israel, etc., and "Far East" for China and Japan. On a globe, measure the distance from your house to Baghdad and Tokyo. Which is nearer? Why should we refer to China and Japan by how far they are from Europe? Why not call them "East Asia"? We might then call Iraq, Israel, and vicinity "Southwest Asia."

Calling Europe a continent itself exemplifies Eurocentrism. A continent is a "large land mass, mostly surrounded by water." By any consistent definition, Asia (or perhaps "Eurasia") is the continent, of which Europe is a peninsula or series of peninsulas (Scandinavia, Iberia, Italy, the Balkans). Yet not only is Europe "a continent," to many it is *the* continent, as in "continental cuisine."

Here exploration is a euphemism for conquest. The "Age of Exploration" or "Age of Discovery" is more accurately called the "Age of Conquest" or "Age of Colonialism." So why do authors use these euphemisms? "Conquest" and "colonizing," which imply violence and force, are much less appealing words than "discovery" or "settlement." Some of the 22 textbooks use the Spanish term "conquistador"—"conqueror" in English—and speak frankly about what Spaniards did to American Indians in Haiti and Mexico. But when authors move to discussing *English* intrusions into the Americas, they revert to headings like "English Settlers Struggle in North America."

During the 1500s and 1600s, what came to be called "the Black Legend" emphasized Spanish mistreatment of American Indians and circulated through England, Holland, France, and other countries. Ironically, while the Spanish treatment of Native Americans was shameful, it was far better than the English. As one textbook, *The American Pageant*, makes clear, "the Spanish paid the Native Americans the high compliment of fusing with them through marriage and incorporating indigenous

Take a Position: Is the "Age of Exploration" Eurocentric?

In what ways is the "Age of Exploration" usually told from a Eurocentric view in American history textbooks? Why? What purposes today are served by doing so? (There are several.)

Explorers don't usually bring along armored attack dogs. Conquistadors do. Columbus brought such dogs on his second voyage, which shows he planned from the beginning to conquer Haiti and the other islands. Las Casas tells how "they take these dogs along with them in all their expeditions, carrying also diverse Indians in chains for them to eat."

culture into their own, rather than shunning and eventually isolating the Indians as their English adversaries would do."

Interestingly, the oldest treatment of Columbus in an American history textbook that I've seen, written in 1830, flatly refers to his "offensive war against the Indians."[16] That is just what it was—a war of conquest. The Spaniards even called themselves "conquistadores." About Columbus, some of today's authors are less accurate than some Livingstone writers in previous centuries. Amnesia seems to have set in.

When authors choose "explore," they also encourage us to identify with Columbus. Perhaps they want us to think of ourselves as part of a grand tradition of white European explorers, a line reaching back through Admiral Peary and Dr. Livingstone to Columbus and Prince Henry the Navigator. It projects into the future with the spaceship *Enterprise* in *Star Trek*, "going boldly where no man [or woman?] has gone before." In some ways, it is a wonderful heroic tradition. But it's not simply a white European tradition. People of all races and cultures took part. Acknowledging their efforts wouldn't make the tradition any less wonderful.

Indeed, Europeans usually depended on the people they "explored." African pilots helped Prince Henry's ship captains learn their way down the coast of Africa. A Native Canadian, William Erasmus, pointed out that in the far north, "explorers you call great men were helpless. They were like lost children, and it was our people who took care of them." When Peary discovered the North Pole, the first person there was not the European American Peary, nor his African American assistant, Matthew Henson, but their four Inuit guides, men and women on whom the entire expedition relied.[17] We have seen how Guacanagarí helped when *Santa María* ran aground. We will see that non-Europeans were also exploring the world long before Columbus. So long as our textbooks hide from us the roles people of color have played in exploration, from 6000 B.C. to the twentieth century, they encourage us to look to Europe and its extensions as the seat of all knowledge about the world.

American Indians or Native Americans?

While we are examining the power of words, what about "Indians"?" Columbus may have thought he had reached the East Indies, China, and Japan, lands of spices and gold. At least he wanted others to believe this. So he called the people "Indians." The name stuck, even though he was off by ten thousand miles. Since the early 1970s, some American Indians in the United States have rejected Columbus's term. They choose to call themselves Native Americans. Others, including the American Indian Movement, choose to stick with American Indians. Today some history books use one, some the other. Because Native people are undecided, I use both.

The peoples of the West Indies were divided into two main groups, Tainos and Caribs, both of whom spoke Arawak. The Caribs raided the Tainos, sometimes taking captives as slaves, and may even have eaten them. "Taino" means "the good people" or "the noble people," which Tainos emphasized to set themselves apart from the Caribs, hoping that the Spanish would treat them as an ally rather than an enemy. Today, a Caribbean indigenous revitalization movement has taken up the name "Taino."[18]

Who Is the Roamer? Who Is the Settler?

Columbus knew that if he could get Europeans to believe that American Indians had no fixed settlements,

16. Henry Trumbull, *History of the Discovery of America; of the Landing of our Forefathers at Plymouth, and of their Most Remarkable Engagements with the Indians in New England From their First Landing in 1620 Until the Final Subjugation of the Natives in 1679* (Boston: George Clark, 1830), 9–11.
17. John Burns, "Canada Tries to Make Restitution to Its Own," *New York Times*, September 1, 1988; "Discoverers' Sons Arrive for Reunion," Burlington (VT) *Free Press*, May 1, 1987; Susan A. Kaplan, "introduction" to *A Black Explorer at the North Pole*, by Matthew Henson (Lincoln: U. of Nebraska Press, 1989).
18. Carl Sauer says "tainos" refers to a social class within the Arawaks. See *The Spanish Main* (Berkeley: U. of California Press, 1966), 37.

then Europeans would agree that Indians had little claim to their land. Therefore, when describing his experiences on Haiti after 1493, he conveniently forgot about their towns and gardens. Now Columbus said they roam about and "live in hills and mountains without fixed settlements." Even today, textbook authors have trouble recognizing that American Indians had settled the Americas. When they imply that Natives didn't really settle here but just roamed, it becomes easier to present the United States as a just and peaceful nation of settlers, rather than usurpers.

Consider Ohio in the 1780s. United States citizens were crossing the Ohio River and squatting on Indian land. Boorstin and Kelley tell how "the Indians raided small parties," which "soon taught the Ohio pioneers to build garrison settlements" like Fort Frye. They title this discussion "New Englanders Settle along the Ohio" and index it as "Indians and settlers in Ohio." The idea that American Indians *were* settlers in Ohio never crossed the authors' or indexer's minds. The new United States fought its first war there, in the 1790s, but the way Boorstin and Kelley present "settlers" versus "Indians," this war seems to be the Indians' fault.[19]

Later we'll see that Columbus *forced* the Arawaks to "live in hills and mountains without fixed settlements." Similarly, in the Ohio Valley in 1795 the United States destroyed the cornfields of the Delawares three times in one year—so the Delawares had to learn to live "without fixed settlements." In Wisconsin and Minnesota the Dakota (Sioux) Indians had been farmers as well. Then a combination of military pressure from the east and the introduction of the horse led them to give up farming, move farther west, and become buffalo hunters.

One textbook, *Life and Liberty*, presents an intriguing pair of illustrations. One shows the famous horse culture of the Plains Indians. The other portrays Indian farmers. *Life and Liberty* then asks, "Which shows Indian life before Europeans arrived and which shows Indian life after? What evidence tells you the date?" Thus, *Life and Liberty* helps students to understand that Europeans did not civilize or settle roaming American Indians. No other book does anything like this. *Pageant* provides the more usual story line: "The Cherokees of Georgia made especially remarkable efforts to learn the ways of the whites. They gradually abandoned their seminomadic

life and adopted a system of settled agriculture." In reality, the Cherokees had been agricultural long before whites arrived.

If we look at history from the Native American viewpoint, we see that to Native eyes *Europeans* were nomads. Native religions relate to places, sacred sites, in land where tribes have lived for millennia. Desert peoples gave rise to book-based religions (Judaism, Christianity, Islam), because they were more nomadic. As Chief Seattle put it in 1855, "To us the ashes of our ancestors are sacred and their resting place is hallowed ground. You wander far from the graves of your ancestors and seemingly without regret."[20] The same could have been said of Columbus.

Textbooks that never call Native Americans settlers now use "settlers" to describe Columbus and the Spanish. "The island of Hispaniola, or Little Spain, was chosen for the first settlement," says *The United States: A History of the Republic*. "Eventually, the settlers established outposts on other islands." "Settlers," though, are usually families, seeking land on which to make permanent new homes. No Spanish women came. Nor did the men intend to stay. Columbus's second expedition was an armed force intended to subdue the Arawaks and take treasure from them. The "settlers" were soldiers and adventurers, accompanied by cannons, guns, crossbows, horses and cavalrymen, and attack dogs in armor. Spaniards saw themselves as soldiers, not settlers, and complained bitterly when asked to do the work of settling.

When Columbus's second voyage reached the West Indies, he started island hopping, looking for the best things to plunder. He was not interested in land. He passed right by the beautiful island of Montserrat because "the Indian women whom we brought with us said that it was not inhabited," he wrote home. But St. Martin "seemed to be worth finding, for judging by the extent of cultivation on it, it appeared very populous." Finally he

Take a Position: Terminology Makes a Difference

The words authors choose influence the positions readers take. Give four examples from this book and tell what difference they make.

---

19. The Ohio war is described by Gary Nash, *Red, White, and Black* (Englewood Cliffs, NJ: Prentice-Hall, 1974), 63, and Francis Jennings, *Empire of Fortune* (New York: Norton, 1988), 63.
20. Chief Seattle, "Our People Are Ebbing Away," in *Great Documents in American Indian History*, ed. Wayne Moquin (New York: Praeger, 1973), 80–83. Rudolf Kaiser discusses this speech in "Chief Seattle's Speech(es)," in *Recovering the Word*, ed. Brian Swann and Arnold Krupat (Berkeley: U. of California Press, 1987), 497–536, esp. 520.

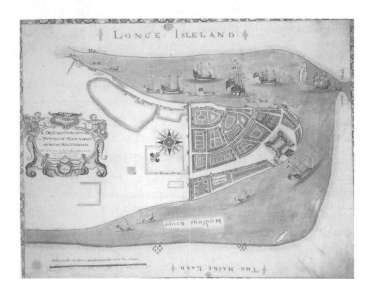

A page before its fable about the "purchase" of Manhattan, *Pageant* includes this illustration of New Amsterdam. Its caption reads, "This drawing clearly shows the tip of Manhattan Island protected by the wall after which Wall Street was named." Whoever wrote the textbook never thought to ask, "Why would the Dutch need a wall, if they bought the whole island fairly?"

chose Haiti because of its large Native population and rumors that they had found gold.[21]

Columbus started a pattern of "settling" where American Indians were most numerous. Everywhere in the Americas, Europeans pitched camp right in the middle of Native populations—Cuzco (Peru), Tenochtitlan (now Mexico City), Natchez (Mississippi), Chicago.

In their treatments of Columbus, most textbooks written after 2000 do admit that he simply took Native land. Later, however, when they reach the story of the United States itself and its predecessor colonies, most books tell a whopper: Native Americans didn't really understand land ownership in the first place. "In their view, the land could not be owned," according to *Pathways to the Present*. "They believed that people had a right to use land or to allow others to use it, but buying or selling land was unthinkable." Nonsense! Natives had roughly the same views about land ownership as Europeans. Both believed a group could sell all of its land, some, or none.[22] Both also believed they could sell while retaining the right to cross unimproved land and hunt and fish on it. Indeed, the ear-

liest Massachusetts courts heard claims by American Indians that the English were violating terms of these land sales by forbidding Natives access that they had guaranteed and letting their pigs molest gardens on Indian soil.

Pageant even repeats the absurd tale of how the Dutch bought Manhattan for $24 worth of beads—"22,000 acres of what is now perhaps the most valuable real estate in the world for pennies per acre."[23] Spinning this

A well-dressed Dutchman hands a string of beads to a Native American wearing only a breechcloth and a full-feathered headdress. Thus, the Dutch bought Manhattan for $24 worth of beads, according to legend. This sculpture, located at the exact spot in lower Manhattan where this transaction never took place, does not strive for realism. If the transaction happened in August, the Dutchman is sweating; if in February, the Native is freezing. No two people have ever been dressed like that on the same spot on the earth on the same day, of course. The artist merely followed a convention about clothing that makes the Indian seem "primitive," the Dutchman "civilized."

21. *Select Letters of Christopher Columbus*, trans. and ed. R.H. Major (New York: Corinth, 1961 [1847]), 82–83.
22. Natives did *not* believe that individuals could sell land, which they held jointly as a group.
23. In 1983, this textbook claimed the Dutch bought Manhattan "from the Indians (who did not actually 'own' it) for trinkets worth about $24—22,000 acres of what is now perhaps the most valuable real estate in the world for one-tenth of a cent per acre." Ironically, purchasing 22,000 acres for $24 *does* amount to about "one-tenth of a cent per acre," not "pennies," so the book was more accurate *before* revision. However, $24 in 1983 bought more than $24 in 2006. Indeed, this is the only $24 *never* to undergo inflation! Imagine how much $24 was in 1630!

yarn legitimizes the conquest: "We didn't simply *take* the land, we *bought* it, fair and square." Unfortunately, it never happened, and the story makes American Indians look foolish. In reality, the Dutch "bought" the rights to Manhattan from the Canarsies for perhaps $2,400 worth of knives, axes, guns, kettles, and blankets. But the Canarsies lived on Long Island! The Dutch warred with the real owners, the Weckquaesgeeks, for years. Finally, around 1644, perhaps with help from the Canarsies, the Dutch exterminated the Weckquaesgeeks.

The Plagues

If Native Americans were about as numerous as Europeans in 1492, how could just a few Europeans conquer and populate America? Europe's advantages in warfare and social technology would have allowed Europeans to dominate the Americas, as they eventually dominated Asia and Africa. Europeans were never able to *settle* China, India, Indonesia, or most of Africa, however. Too many people already lived there. Why were the Americas different? How could Spain, a country of only 5 million people, take over Mexico, a country of 25 million?

Disease was by far the biggest single factor. From Haiti to Plymouth Rock, disastrous epidemics among Native Americans made it easier for Europeans to take over. In 1617, for example, just before the Pilgrims landed, a plague struck New England that made the Black Death in Europe pale by comparison. Today we think this disease was the bubonic plague, although smallpox and influenza are also candidates. British fishermen probably gave it to them, without meaning to. Within three years this plague wiped out between 90 and 96 percent of the inhabitants of coastal New England. The Native societies lay devastated.

Europe, Asia, and Africa have historically been the breeding ground for most human illnesses. Humans are tropical creatures that evolved in Africa. Tropical diseases evolved along with them. When people moved to cooler climates, many diseases had trouble moving. If archaeologists are correct, humans migrated to the Americas from Siberia, by boat or on foot. Many germs must have met their death on that frigid trip. Thus, the first settlers in the Western Hemisphere arrived in a healthier condition than any people on earth have enjoyed before or after. Not keeping cows, pigs, horses, or chickens kept them healthy, because livestock and humans pass many diseases back and forth. Ironically, their very health now proved their undoing, for they had built up no resistance, genetically or through exposure during childhood, to the microbes that Europeans and Africans brought with them.[24]

Only "the twentieth person is scarce left alive," wrote British eyewitness Robert Cushman, describing a death rate unknown in all previous human experience.[25] The plague killed every single person in the town of Patuxet, Massachusetts. Because nearby American Indian tribes were also much reduced in population, they allowed the Pilgrims to settle right in Patuxet and use its cornfields. After all, no one else was. The Pilgrims renamed it Plymouth.

Thus, the plague made history—but not always our history books! How authors treat this plague—and all the other plagues that depopulated the Americas, Hawaii, Tahiti, other islands, and Australia—can tell us how history gets written, well and badly. The oldest American history in my library, J.W. Barber's *Interesting Events in the History of the United States*, published in 1829, told the truth about the plague of 1617: "Whole towns were depopulated. The living were not able to bury the dead; and their bodies were found lying above ground, many years after. The Massachusetts Indians are said to have been reduced from 30,000 to 300 fighting men."

What do we learn of this plague in today's books? As of 1992, almost nothing. (However, we shall see that the situation has changed in books published more recently.) Only three of the original fifteen textbooks I studied, all published before that date, even mention disease as a factor at Plymouth or anywhere in New England. The rest prefer to attribute the Pilgrims' success to their character—they had "just the right combination of hopes and fears, optimism and pessimism, self-confidence and humility to be successful settlers," in the words of Boorstin and Kelley. Another case of amnesia in our history books—we used to know all about it, then we forgot.

24. William H. McNeill, lecture at the U. of Vermont, October 18, 1988; Crosby, *The Columbian Exchange*, 34–37; Peter Farb, *Man's Rise to Civilization* (New York: Avon, 1968), 42–43; Hubbert M. Schnurrenberger, *Diseases Transmitted from Animals to Man* (Springfield, IL: Charles C. Thomas, 1975). See also Alfred W. Crosby, *Ecological Imperialism: The Biological Expansion of Europe, 900–1900* (New York: Cambridge U. Press, 1976), 31. Andeans do have llamas. The Andes may be too high and cold to promote disease among llamas or people, however.
25. Simpson gives a readable account of this plague in *Invisible Armies*. Cushman is quoted in Charles M. Segal and David C. Stineback, *Puritans, Indians, and Manifest Destiny* (New York: Putnam's, 1977), 54–55. See also Neal Salisbury, "Red Puritans: The 'Praying Indians' of Massachusetts Bay and John Eliot," in *Race Relations in British North America, 1607–1783*, ed. Bruce A. Glasrud and Alan M. Smith (Chicago: Nelson-Hall, 1982), 44. However, Dobyns believes this plague swept up the Atlantic coast all the way from Florida. See *Their Number Become Thinned*.

This Aztec art shows an Aztec dying from smallpox. Only one textbook published between 1974 and 1992 included any image of American Indian disease. Three of the six books published after 2000 include this image, which their authors may have seen in *Lies My Teacher Told Me*, which first came out in 1994. The other three at least tell of the extent of the diseases in words, sometimes quite effectively.

Like the Pilgrims, the Spanish were also aided by epidemics. When Cortés marched into Tenochtitlan in triumph, dead Aztecs were everywhere. A smallpox epidemic had laid low the defenders of the city. "We could not walk without treading on the bodies and heads of dead Indians," wrote a historian with Cortés.

These plagues are the most important event in the entire history of the Americas, because they allowed Europeans to settle, not just conquer. The epidemics continue to this very day among the Natives in the Amazon basin. In the 1980s, miners and loggers reached the Yanomamos of northern Brazil and southern Venezuela, bringing European diseases. A fourth of their total population died in just one year, 1989. In 2009, a swine flu epidemic killed more. A year later, malaria killed at least 50 more.[26]

Before 1992, most of our histories avoided telling us about these plagues too. Rather, they created a mythic past. They omitted how 25 million people in Mexico were reduced to fewer than 2 million a century later. They left out how perhaps 14 million Natives in the United States were cut down to just 200,000. Instead, they told how our brave European ancestors conquered a virgin wilderness. Indeed, *American Adventures* titled its chapter about the first British settlers in North America "Opening the Wilderness."

It's hard to believe that the neglect of this topic in textbooks published before 1992 resulted from ignorance. After all, J.W. Barber put it in his book in 1829! Moreover, primary sources told about the plagues from the start. John Winthrop, for example, governor of Massachusetts Bay Colony, called the plague "miraculous." To a friend in England in 1634, he wrote:

> But for the natives in these parts, God hath so pursued them, as for 300 miles space the greatest part of them are swept away by the smallpox which still continues among them. So as God hath thereby cleared our title to this place, those who remain in these parts, being in all not 50, have put themselves under our protection.[27]

Nevertheless, many authors remained ignorant. In 1990, while working on *Lies My Teacher Told Me*, I asked John Garraty, author of one of the textbooks I was studying, why he did not even mention the plague in Massachusetts. He replied, honestly, "Until today, I didn't know about it." Two years later, he included it as the first item in his book *1,001 Things Everyone Should Know About American History*. So Garraty had no vested interest to keep readers in the dark; he simply did not know better. He only wrote what he knew.

We shall see later that the people listed as authors often did not write the books with their names on them. Even if they did, most writers include only what they know. They do not do much new research before writing new history textbooks. Each historian has specialized. Imagine that you and I agree to write a U.S. history textbook together. Imagine that you're an expert on women's roles in the Great Depression, while I'm expert on race relations in the twentieth century. Neither of us knows much about Columbus. Let's suppose you lose the coin flip and get to write about Columbus. Of course, you could take several days, read three or four secondary works on Columbus and colonization, maybe read what we have of his journal, and then bang out the two pages we need on Columbus's voyages.[28] But that would take work. Instead, the publisher, trying to be helpful, has sent us several competitors' books, so you take a short cut and rewrite what they say, along with what you remember

26. James Brooke, "For an Amazon Indian Tribe, Civilization Brings Mostly Disease and Death," *New York Times*, December 24, 1989; "Isolated Amazon Indians Die in 'Swine Flu Epidemic,'" *Survival International*, November 4, 2009, survivalinternational.org/news/5173 (accessed September 2013); "Amazon Indians Hit by Deadly Epidemic in Venezuela," *Daily Caller*, dailycaller.com/2010/10/30/amazon-indians-hit-by-deadly-epidemic-in-venezuela/#ixzz2eJQDx8DQ (accessed September 2013).

27. Quoted in Simpson, *Invisible Armies*, 7.

28. Secondary works are books by scholars, usually written well afterward, that in turn are usually based on primary sources—journals, drawings, and other items from the time.

from college, long ago. Perhaps that explains this similarity between two treatments of the flat earth myth, the first from Boorstin and Kelley, the second from *The American Journey*.

He altered the records of distances they had covered so the crew would not think they had gone too far from home.	To convince the crew that they had not traveled too far from home, Columbus altered the distances in the ship's log.

Unfortunately, we shall see that real research reveals the whole story to be hokum.

Textbooks Change in Response to 1992

In the late 1990s, there was a sea change in what "everybody" knew about Columbus. The new textbooks I studied, written after 2000, reflect this change: all of them discuss the epidemics that led to the populating of the Americas by Europeans and Africans.

Why this change? I would like to claim credit for it, and surely I *did* tell at least one author—Garraty—about the importance of disease at Plymouth. *Lies My Teacher Told Me* did become a bestseller, and editors at textbook publishers did hear about it. Honestly, though, I think the real mover of opinion about Columbus was the series of dramatic events that took place in 1992 across the United States.

It was the Columbian Quincentenary—half a millennium since Columbus reached the Western Hemisphere. It was supposed to be a grand celebration. After all, the 400th anniversary had prompted the largest world's fair in history (the Columbian Exposition in Chicago), a statue in New York City's Central Park, a postage stamp, and exultant ceremonies across the United States. For 1992, President George H. W. Bush appointed 50 committees to spearhead celebrations in each state. "Christopher Columbus not only opened the door to a New World," Bush announced, "but also set an example for us all by showing what monumental feats can be accomplished through perseverance and faith."

A funny thing happened on the way to the celebration: uninvited guests crashed the party. In Washington, D.C., demonstrators splashed the huge Columbus sculpture in front of Union Station with red paint, leaving the message "500 years of genocide." In Denver, the American

Doing History: How Textbooks Change

Compare two versions of the same textbook, one written before 1992, one after 2000, about the Columbian Exchange. Or compare the book you use with one of the better textbooks on this topic, such as *Holt American Nation* or *The American Pageant*.

Indian Movement put up a "countermemorial," consisting of one hundred skeletal tepees, burned and scorched, accompanied by 29 official-looking historical markers with texts by Native American leaders. Columbus statues collected red paint and "murderer" graffiti from Boston and Newport, Rhode Island, to Pittsburgh and on to California. Protests have continued every October since then. As well, an outpouring of new scholarship, including bestselling popular books, injected the "Columbian Exchange" into our national vocabulary. This is the process, started by Columbus, of crops, animals, gold and silver, diseases, and ideas crossing the oceans regularly. (The poster shows the Exchange visually.) Disease made up perhaps the most important single element of the Exchange. After 1992, even the nameless clerks who write many history textbooks learned of it. The entire process teaches us that public acts, even actions in the streets, can influence history—the stories we tell ourselves about the past.

Learning Was a Two-Way Street

Having concocted a wilderness, textbook authors next created a frontier between "civilization" and "the wilderness."[29] No such frontier existed. In reality, Europeans dominated one area, American Indians another, with contested land between them. Some Indians lived with Europeans, beginning with some Arawak women on Haiti who married Spaniards. Some Europeans lived with Indians, often marrying into tribes and sometimes becoming leaders. European and Native societies both acculturated—each learned from the other. Columbus started the process. Beginning with his first voyage, he brought back ideas and products from the Arawaks. A later section will tell how these American exports affected Africa and Eurasia.

Sadly, this is not the story most of our textbooks tell. We have seen that authors marginalize American Indians from the start, leaving out their role in the Columbus

---

29. To their credit, not all textbooks now say "wilderness."

story. Then they underestimate Native population and fail to mention how Europeans moved directly into Native cities and town sites. Logically, they cannot then give much attention to how American Indian cultures influenced "white" culture. Terms like "primitive" and "wilderness" block them from imagining that Europeans had much to learn from those they settled among.

EXPLORATION BEFORE COLUMBUS

After American Indians, the next people to reach the Americas certainly were not the Spanish. Long before Columbus sailed to America, explorers from Africa, Asia, and Europe almost surely reached our shores. Since the books emphasize the uniqueness of Columbus's achievement, however, they downplay his predecessors.

The books do admit that Columbus didn't start from scratch. Every textbook account of the European exploration of the Americas begins with Prince Henry the Navigator, of Portugal, between 1415 and 1460. Authors portray Henry as discovering Madeira and the Azores. But Henry seems to have started from scratch. Authors seem unaware that long ago people from Phoenicia (now Lebanon, Israel, and Syria) and Egypt sailed at least as far as Madeira and the Azores and traded with the aboriginal inhabitants of the Canary Islands. The textbooks credit Bartolomeu Dias for first rounding the Cape of Good Hope at the southern tip of Africa in 1488, even though the Africans and Phoenicians had sailed all the way around Africa two thousand years earlier.

Omitting the accomplishments of these Afro-Phoenicians is ironic, because Prince Henry himself

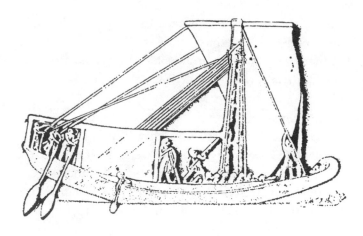

This ancient Egyptian ship provided a model for Thor Heyerdahl, who sailed a replica across the Atlantic in the 1970s. He tells the fascinating story in *The Ra Expeditions* (Garden City, NY: Doubleday, 1971). Heyerdahl's *Early Man and the Ocean* (New York: Vintage, 1980) discusses the debate between those who believe people crossed the seas long ago and those who don't.

knew about them. Indeed, his knowledge of their feats inspired him to imitate them. Textbooks don't tell us this, however. It doesn't fit with their overall story line. They want to report how "we" (white Europeans) taught "them" (the rest of the world) how to do things. Readers are left to wonder how, without "our" help, Eskimos ever reached Greenland, Polynesians ever reached Madagascar, or Afro-Phoenicians ever reached the Canaries![30]

Authors View Modern Technology as a European Development

By treating ocean travel as the invention of Europeans, U.S. history textbooks encourage us to think that nobody sailed the oceans before the Portuguese. "The Portuguese designed a new kind of sailing ship—the 'caravel,'" Boorstin and Kelley tell us. The textbooks also show Henry inventing navigation for the first time. They imply that before Europe there was nothing, at least nothing worth knowing.

In fact, Henry was mostly collecting ideas from ancient Egypt, Phoenicia, China, and India—ideas, moreover, that then got developed further in Arabia and North Africa. These ideas included charts of the stars and names of the constellations from Arab cultures. Navigation instruments such as the astrolabe came from the Middle East. The compass was Chinese. Arabic numerals, making math easier, came to Europe from Arabs but began in India. Even the word "caravel" derives from Arabic; Arab

---

Take a Position: Of What Importance Is the Distant Past?

What difference does it make whether African navigators got to the Americas? Whether Afro-Phoenicians circumnavigated Africa? Whether Egypt was "white" or "black" or interracial (and not color conscious)? Whether mankind originated in Africa or Southeast Asia or the Americas? (Or choose your own controversy from the distant past.)

---

30. Constance Irwin, *Fair Gods and Stone Faces* (New York: St. Martin's, 1963), 193–211, 217, 241; Cyrus Gordon, *Before Columbus* (New York: Crown, 1971), 119–25; Geoffrey Ashe et al., *The Quest for America* (London: Pall Mall, 1971), 78–79.

seamen had used caravels for several centuries in the eastern Mediterranean.[31]

Cultures don't usually develop all by themselves. Rather, diffusion of ideas is the most important cause of cultural development. Contact with other cultures often triggers a cultural flowering, called "syncretism." We learn in elementary school that Persian civilization flowered long ago, due to its location on the Tigris and Euphrates rivers and the fact that its territory was crisscrossed by overland trade routes. Thus, the Persians benefited from contact with other societies. Textbook authors have a golden opportunity to apply this same idea of cultural diffusion to Henry at the dawn of European world domination. Unfortunately, they squander it.[32]

This is another case of texts being Eurocentric. Authors see European culture as more advanced than any other, so they leave out the fact that Europe got many of its ideas from other cultures.

The First Explorers Were American Indians

Textbooks do tell us about the first explorers. Native Americans got here on foot, they say. During the most recent Ice Age, between about 26,000 B.P. (Before the Present), and 12,000 B.P., so much water was frozen in glaciers that the worldwide sea level dropped. People were able to walk across the Bering Strait from Siberia to Alaska.

While this may have happened, it's not the full story. Archaeologists simply aren't sure how or when the Americas got populated.

Archaeology Is Not Dead

One way archaeologists learn about the past is by studying how people today differ from or resemble each other. Most Native Americans, from Argentina to Canada, share one blood type (O) and some other genetic similarities. Therefore, some physical archaeologists believe that most of the millions of people in the Americas in 1492 descended from one small band. Such a small group might have crossed the Bering Strait by boat or on a longer voyage across the Pacific.

Other archaeologists think that several groups of people walked across the strait, perhaps at very different times. Some archaeologists believe that the first people arrived about 12,000 B.P. Others keep finding man-made objects in the Americas that they date to 30,000 B.P. or even 70,000 B.P. No land route connected Alaska to Siberia then. Another controversy concerns "Clovis points," a style of arrowheads and spearheads first found in New Mexico that have since been found all over North America. But Clovis-style points have not been found in Siberia, while they have been found in Iberia! Yet another possibility is that millions of people may have lived in the Americas long before 13,000 years ago. We don't know for sure. Archaeology provides more questions than answers. That's what makes it such an interesting field of study—archaeologists don't know all the answers. Lamentably, history textbooks are more comfortable with answers than uncertainties. Their treatments of the first 12,000 to 70,000 years of human history in the Americas suffer as a result. Archaeologists study people of long ago, but the field is alive with controversy.[33] Besides the issues of dating the first arrivals, some scientists believe that a comet or huge meteor hit the earth's atmosphere above Canada and exploded about 13,000 B.P. It may have killed almost all humans (except those in caves), as well as most large animals (mastodons, giant sloths, etc.). If true, then we need to look for very different civilizations before and after that catastrophe.[34]

Most textbooks ignore all these issues and simply pick a date for the arrival of the first people, usually 12,000 B.P. Thus, they present archaeology as a dead discipline. A new book, *The American Journey*, first published in 2000, is perhaps the worst offender. It claims that archaeologists' "most recent discoveries show that the Native Americans" walked across "a stretch of land called Beringia that once joined Asia and the Americas." Sadly, this is the old traditional answer. It is precisely archaeologists' "most recent discoveries" that call this tradition into question. About these recent discoveries, *Journey* says not a word. I suspect that's because *Journey* is based on older textbooks, not current sources.

31. Abbas Hamdni, "An Islamic Background to the Voyages of Discovery," in *The Legacy of Muslim Spain*, ed. Salma Jayussi (Leiden: E.J. Brill, 1994), 289–90.

32. One textbook, *American Adventure*, points out "the magnetic compass had come from China," and "from the Arabs came an instrument called the astrolabe." *The American People* mentions that the "lateen-rigged caravel [was] adapted from a Moorish ship design." Otherwise, all these histories present the Portuguese achievements as new inventions on the face of the globe.

33. For a lively account of the issues, see Marc Stengel, "The Diffusionists Have Landed," *Atlantic Monthly*, January 2000, 35–48, theatlantic.com/issues/2000/01/001stengel.htm. Students can bring Stengel up to date with careful Web research.

34. Enrico de Lazaro, "Topper Site Supports Theory of Extraterrestrial Impact 12,900 Years Ago," 9/20/2012 sci-news.com/archaeology/article00599.html; "Comet theory collides with Clovis research, may explain disappearance of ancient people," U. of SC website, 6/28/2007, uscnews.sc.edu/ARCH190.html.

One book, *The American Adventure*, is different. It begins by admitting uncertainty: "This page may be out of date by the time it is read." It continues by presenting competing claims that humans have been in the Americas for 12,000, 21,000, or 40,000 years. As a result, although *Adventure* is the oldest of the books I reviewed, its pre-Columbian pages have *not* gone out of date.[35]

Some Natives Did Not Walk to America

Whether 70,000 years ago or 12,000, the first expedition of Asians to America was not the only one. Native Americans came in at least three waves. First came the basic group that wound up diffused from the Micmacs

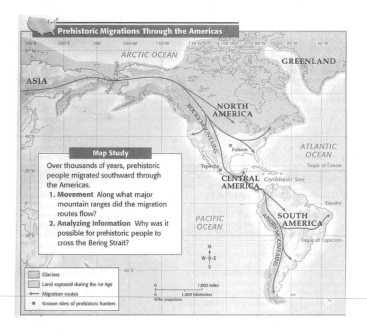

Five of the six most recent textbooks I analyzed include maps like this, from *The American Journey*, that show "the" route the first settlers of the Americas took to get here. (The sixth has no map but says the same thing in words.) *Journey* goes on, "From the north, the migrants gradually moved into new territory. They spread out across the Americas, going as far east as the Atlantic Ocean and as far south as the tip of South America." We don't know this, however. Archaeological finds do not get older as we go up through the Yukon and cross Alaska. No evidence suggests that migration routes "flowed" along any mountain ranges. To be sure, absence of evidence is not evidence of absence. Archaeologists have not done enough excavation in northwestern North America. Nevertheless, it may be more likely that migration "flowed" along the seacoast, by canoe and small boat. However, since the seacoast then may have been miles to the west of the seacoast now, no archaeological evidence supports boat travel either.

in Nova Scotia to the Yaghans at the bottom of South America. We know they had boats, because they reached islands off California. Then a group called Dené arrived, perhaps 10,000 to 2,500 B.P. They settled in northern Canada. Some made it to Arizona and New Mexico around 1000 A.D., where they got called Apaches and Navajos. Inuits or Eskimos arrived by kayaks beginning perhaps 9,000 to 2,000 B.P. They never stopped coming and have kept in touch with relatives in Siberia ever since.

Not one U.S. history textbook suggests that American Indians might have come by boat. *The American Journey* even writes, "Some scientists think that the Inuit were the last migrants to cross the land bridge into North America." Presumably they portaged their kayaks as they walked across! Notice also the two questions that the map asks. They are typical regurgitation items. Students are supposed to read "Rocky Mountains" and "Andes Mountains" on the map and parrot them back to answer #1. Students are also supposed to parrot back that Beringia made it possible to walk across to America.

Actually, early people had boats. In fact, people probably had boats before they were people! *Homo erectus*, an evolutionary predecessor of us, *Homo sapiens*, probably reached Flores, in eastern Indonesia, 800,000 years ago. No matter how much ice piled up during an ice age, you could never walk to Flores. So *Homo erectus* must have had boats.

Even today, it's only 56 miles across the Bering Strait; on a clear day, people on either side can climb a hill and see across! There are even two islands at the halfway point to make crossing easier! It's harder to walk 56 miles than to paddle or sail, especially if you have to cut a trail as the first traveler. Nevertheless, ocean navigation doesn't fit in with the textbooks' story line—that American Indians were primitive. Walking is more primitive than boat building and navigation. Therefore, even though they got here first, Natives aren't pictured as explorers in our textbooks.

Explorers from Africa, Asia, and Europe Probably Beat Columbus to America

No book sets Columbus in the context of pre-Columbian explorers. Instead, they maintain that the Americas remained isolated before Columbus. As *American History* puts it, "For thousands of years these tribal societies knew nothing of the rest of the world. They were

---

35. Although refusing to give up the usual "know-it-all" textbook tone, one other text, *A History of the Republic*, does tell of uncertainty in archaeology.

18

as isolated from their original homeland in Asia and from Europe and Africa as if they were on the moon." Repeated arrivals from cultures around the globe don't fit in with this story line. We shall see that American histories want to glorify Columbus. Omitting his predecessors makes Columbus's feat look all the more impressive.

In a way, Columbus's famous 1492 expedition was the last in a series of voyages to and from the Americas. Table 1 gives a chronological list of explorers who may have reached the Americas before Columbus, with comments on the quality of evidence for each. New findings in the future may confirm or disprove some of these possibilities, as archaeologists and historians compare American cultures and cultures in Africa, Europe, and Asia.[36]

Keeping up with this new evidence is a lot of work. Sheer laziness may help to explain why authors leave out explorers to the Americas before Columbus. You can't teach what you don't know. To tell about earlier explorers, authors would first have to learn about them. This takes work. To do a good job, authors would have to read at least the works cited in the preceding footnote. They would also have to introduce their readers to uncertainties and controversies, rather than just give answers. We have seen that authors don't really do much research before writing their textbooks. It's easier to imitate existing textbooks and just retell the old familiar Columbus story.

Textbooks Downplay the Vikings

Most history books do mention the Norse. These daring sailors reached America in a series of voyages across the North Atlantic, first setting up communities on the Faeroe Islands, Iceland, and Greenland. The Norse colony on

36. How good is the evidence for these predecessors of Columbus? These sources can help you can make up your own mind. Bear in mind, however, that they may already be out of date. New finds keep on happening. For example, archaeologists may have found human footprints in central Mexico that date to 40,000 B.P.

General books: John L. Sorenson and Martin H. Raish have compiled an enormous bibliography, *Pre-Columbian Contact with the Americas Across the Oceans* (Provo, UT: Research Press, 1990), with pro and con listings on each topic. Cf. Sorenson, *Mormon's Codex* (Salt Lake City, UT: Deseret, 2013). Kenneth Feder attacks many diffusionist claims in *Frauds, Myths, and Mysteries* (New York: McGraw-Hill, 2013 [1990]). For Iberia: Dennis Stanford and Bruce A. Bradley, *Across Atlantic Ice* (Berkeley: U. of California Press, 2012).

For Indonesia: Stephen C. Jett, "The Development and Distribution of the Blowgun," *Annals of the Association of American Geographers* (Davis, CA: U. of California, 1970). Similar manufacture of paper: Paul Tolstoy, "Paper Route," *Natural History*, June 1991, 6–14; and *Feats and Wisdom of the Ancients* (Alexandria, VA: Time-Life, 1990), 122. Cf. Carroll Riley et al., *Man Across the Sea* (Austin: U. of Texas Press, 1971), especially the article by Jett, Sorenson, and Raish, #H255, M109, and S57.

For Japanese: Betty J. Meggers, "Did Japanese Fishermen Really Reach Ecuador 5000 Years Ago?" *Early Man 2* (1980): 15–19, and "Contacts from Asia," in *The Quest for America*, by Geoffrey Ashe et al., 239–59. Cf. *Feats and Wisdom of the Ancients*, 124.

For Athabascans, Navajos, and Inuits: William Fitzhugh, "Crossroads of Continents: Review and Prospect," in *Proceedings of the Crossroads Symposium*, ed. Fitzhugh and V. Chaussonet (Washington: Smithsonian Institution, 1988). Cf. Ian Stevenson, *Twenty Cases Suggestive of Reincarnation* (Charlottesville: U. of Virginia Press, 1974), 218–19.

For Chinese: Joseph Needham and Lu Gwei-Djen, *Trans-Pacific Echoes and Resonances* (Singapore: World Scientific, 1985); Paul Shao, *The Origin of Ancient American Cultures* (Ames: Iowa State U. Press, 1983); *Feats and Wisdom of the Ancients*, 121; *Twenty Cases Suggestive of Reincarnation*, 218–19; Constance Irwin, *Fair Gods and Stone Faces*, 249–51; Sorenson and Raish, #L228, 231, 238–41 et al.; Masao Uchibayashi, "Maize in Pre-Columbian China," Yakugaku Zasshi, 125 #7 (2005), 583–86; Theodore Schurr, "Tracking Genes through Time and Space," in Robson Bonnichsen et al., eds., *Paleoamerican Origins: Beyond Clovis* (College Station: Texas A&M U. Press, 2005), 228; Gavin Menzies, *1421* (New York: HarperCollins, 2004 [2002]).

For Afro-Phoenicians: Alexander von Wuthenau, *The Art of Terracotta Pottery in Pre-Columbian Central and South America* (New York: Crown, 1970) and *Unexpected Faces in Ancient America* (New York: Crown, 1975). Cf. Ivan Van Sertima, *They Came Before Columbus* (New York: Random House, 1976); Thor Heyerdahl, "The Bearded Gods Speak," in *The Quest for America*, 199–238; *Feats and Wisdom of the Ancients*, 123; Irwin, *Fair Gods and Stone Faces*, 67–71, 89–96, 122–45, 176–86; and Sorenson and Raish, #J13-17, G71 et al.

For Celts: Barry Fell, *America BC* (New York: Quadrangle, 1976) and *Saga America* (New York: Times Books, 1980).

For Irish: *The Quest for America*, 24–48. Cf. Gunnar Thompson, "press release, U. of Hawaii," March, 15, 1996.

For Norse: Erik Wahlgren, *The Vikings and America* (New York: Thames & Hudson, 1986).

For Polynesians: Richard Jantz and Douglas Owsley, "Circumpacific Populations and the Peopling of the New World," in Bonnichsen, 267–75.

For West Africans: Samuel Marble, *Before Columbus* (Cranbury, NJ: Barnes, 1980), 22–25. Cf. *They Came Before Columbus*; Arthur E. Morgan, *Nowhere Was Somewhere*, 198; Michael Anderson Bradley, *Dawn Voyage* (Toronto: Summer Hill Press, 1987); and Sorenson and Raish, #H344.

For Portuguese: *Before Columbus*, 25. Cf. *They Came Before Columbus*; *Nowhere Was Somewhere*, 197; *The Quest for America*; David Quinn, *England and the Discovery of America, 1481–1620* (New York: Knopf, 1974), 41–43, 85–86; and H.Y. Oldham, "A Pre-Columbian Discovery of America," *Geographical Journal 3* (1895): 221–33.

For Basques: Jack Forbes, *Black Africans and Native Americans* (Oxford: Basil Blackwell, 1988), 20; cf. Mark Kurlansky, *The Basque History of the World* (New York: Penguin, 2001).

For Bristol fishers: Quinn, *England and the Discovery of America, 1481–1620*, 5–105. Cf. A.A. Ruddock, "John Day of Bristol," *Geographical Journal 132* (1966): 225–33; Robert Blow, *Abroad in America* (New York: Continuum, 1990), 17; G.R. Crone, *The Discovery of America* (New York: Weybright & Talley, 1960), 157–58; and Carl Sauer, *Sixteenth-Century North America* (Berkeley: U. of California Press, 1971), 6.

Table 1. Explorers to America Before Columbus

Year	From	To	Quality of Evidence
70,000?–12,000? B.C.	Siberia	Alaska	Certain: the survivors peopled the Americas
70,000?–9000? B.C. (via Aleutians?)	Australia	Chilé	Low: DNA research still needed in South America
16,000? B.C.–12,000 B.C.	Iberia	New England	Low: similar way to flake stone tools
5000?–500? B.C.	Indonesia	South America (or other direction)	Moderate: similar blowguns, paper-making, sweet potatoes, etc.
3100? B.C., c.500? B.C.	Japan	Ecuador	Moderate: similar pottery, fishing styles
9000?–1000? B.C.	Siberia	Canada, New Mexico	Certain: Navajos, Apaches, and Athabaskans resemble each other culturally, yet differ from other Native Americans
9000? B.C. to present	Siberia	Alaska	Certain: continuing contact by Inuits across Bering Strait
3000? B.C.–500 B.C., 450? A.D., 1421 A.D.	China	Central America	Moderate: Chinese legend, cultural similarities, DNA among Mayans, inference from old maps
c.2000 B.C.–300 A.D.	Afro-Phoenicia	Central America	Moderate: Negroid and Caucasoid likenesses in sculpture and ceramics, Arab history, nicotine in mummies, etc.
500 B.C.	Phoenicians, Celts	New England, perhaps elsewhere	Low: similarities in stone structures and what may be writing
600 A.D.	Ireland, via Iceland	Newfoundland? West Indies?	Low: legends of St. Brendan, written c. 850 A.D., confirmed by Norse sagas
1000–1350	Greenland, Iceland	Labrador, Baffin Land, Newfoundland, Nova Scotia, possibly New England	Certain: oral sagas, confirmed by archaeology on Newfoundland
1304?–1424?	Polynesia	Chilé	Moderate: chicken bones precede Spanish; similar fishhooks and plants
1311?–1460?	W. Africa	Haiti, Panama, possibly Brazil	Moderate: Portuguese sources in West Africa, Columbus on Haiti, Balboa in Panama
c.1460	Portugal	Newfoundland? Brazil?	Low: inference from cryptic Portuguese sources
1375?–1491	Basque Spain	Newfoundland coast	Low: cryptic historical sources
1481–91	Bristol, England	Newfoundland coast	Low: cryptic historical sources
1492	Spain	Caribbean, including Hispaniola	Certain: historical sources

Greenland lasted 500 years, about as long as the European settlement of the Americas from 1492 until now. From Greenland a series of expeditions, some planned, some accidental, reached various parts of North America, including Baffin Land, Labrador, Newfoundland, and possibly New England.

Textbooks minimize the Viking expeditions. *American Journey* writes, "Leif Eriksson got lost on his way to Greenland and landed in present-day Newfoundland. He established a small settlement there, but it did not last." Actually, in about 1005, Thorfinn and Gudrid Karlsefni led a party of 65 or 165 or 265 homesteaders (the old Norse sagas vary), with livestock and supplies, to settle "Vineland." They lasted two years. Gudrid gave birth to a son. Then continuing conflict with Native Americans caused them to give up. But this trip was not an isolated incident: Norse were still exporting wood from Labrador to Greenland 350 years later. Some archaeologists and historians believe that the Norse got as far down the coast as North Carolina. Columbus surely learned of Greenland and probably North America if he visited Iceland in 1477, as he claimed he did.[37]

Who Should Be Included? Why?

"So what?" might nonetheless be one response to the Vikings. While textbooks like *American Journey* minimize the Vikings' experiences, it's probably fair to say that their voyages didn't make much difference to the fate of the world. The Norse didn't merge with or influence Native cultures. Their knowledge of America, while not lost in Europe, made little impact there.

So should texts leave them out? Is impact on the present the only reason for including an event or fact? Of course not—our history textbooks would shrink to twenty pages! We include the Norse voyages, not for their geopolitical significance, but because including them gives a more complete picture of the past. Moreover, comparing the Norse voyages to Columbus's second voyage would help students understand the changes that took place in Europe between 1000 and 1493. As we shall see, Columbus's second voyage was ten times larger than the Norse attempts at settling. This new European ability to mobilize caused Columbus's voyages to take on their awesome significance. Besides all that, the Norse make for a wonderful story of seafaring skill, illustrating human possibility.

EUROCENTRISM AFFECTS WHAT TEXTBOOKS INCLUDE AND EXCLUDE

Most textbooks totally omit explorers before Columbus other than the Norse. Although seafarers from Africa and Asia probably made it to the Americas, they rarely make it into the history books.

The Afro-Phoenicians

The most famous are the possible voyages by Afro-Phoenicians, probably launched from Morocco but ultimately from Lebanon and Egypt. They may have ended up on the Atlantic coast of Mexico in about 750 B.C. Along the eastern coast of Mexico stand colossal rock heads that date to around 750 B.C. An archaeologist who helped uncover them called them "amazingly Negroid," but most archaeologists today disagree. However, anthropologist Ivan Van Sertima claims "the features are

This basalt head, nine feet tall, is in southeastern Mexico and dates to 750 B.C. Some archaeologists think the face looks like a naturalistic portrait of an African. Other archaeologists believe that the mouth lines resemble expressions Mayan children still make. Still others think the statues are of "fat babies" or American Indian kings.

---

37. For the Norse, William W. Fitzhugh and Elisabeth I. Ward, eds. *Vikings: The North Atlantic Saga* (Washington: Smithsonian Institution Press, 2000). Cf. Forbes, *Black Africans and Native Americans*, 19. The Norse findings were known in Europe, according to James Duff, *The Truth About Columbus* (London: Jarrolds, 1937), 9–13.

This photo of a ceramic head appears in Alexander von Wuthenau's book *Unexpected Faces in Ancient America*. He identifies it as a "beautiful distinguished Semitic head from Veracruz," because its features look Caucasian, even Semitic, like people from Lebanon, Syria, and Israel. Pre-Columbian Natives had no beards, only a few facial hairs, which they plucked. Archaeologists point out that von Wuthenau's collection was not gathered scientifically, so his heads have not been well dated. If even one is genuine, however, and predates Columbus, it poses a problem for traditional anthropology.[38]

not only Negro-African in type but individual in their facial particulars." American Indians also created what seem to be Negro and Caucasian faces in small ceramic figures like the face shown below.

Van Sertima and others have found other evidence for the presence of Africans and Caucasians in the Americas. For instance, looms and other cultural elements are very similar on both sides of the Atlantic. Skeletons dated well before 1492 have been identified as probably Negroid. Information from African history tells about extensive ocean navigation by Africans and Phoenicians around 750 B.C. Some diseases found in Africans have been identified in pre-Columbian corpses in Brazil. Conversely, some Egyptian mummies contain traces of nicotine and cocaine, from tobacco and coca—plants native to the Americas.

We Use History to Prove Things About Ourselves

What is the importance today of these possible African and Phoenician predecessors of Columbus? Like the Vikings, they provide a fascinating story. We might also realize another kind of importance by thinking about the

meaning of Columbus Day to Italian Americans. When he proclaimed Columbus Day in 1989, President George H.W. Bush said, "Americans of Italian and Spanish descent will have special reason to join." In celebrating Columbus Day, Italian Americans and by extension other European Americans are saying, "Look at us! *We* did this in history." It's no accident that movie star Gina Lollobrigida and baseball great Joe DiMaggio, both of Italian origin, starred in New York City's Columbus Day parade in 1991. DiMaggio called Columbus Day "absolutely good." Thus he showed pride in his heritage, if not much knowledge of Columbus.

Scandinavians and Scandinavian Americans always believed the Norse oral sagas about the Vikings, even when most historians didn't. Similarly, African Americans who have seen the statues and ceramics in Mexico feel proud that their ancestors probably made it to the Americas long before Columbus. Van Sertima's book *They Came Before Columbus* has gone through printing after printing. Rap music groups chant "but we already had been there" in verses about Columbus.[39] Obviously African Americans, like Italian Americans and Scandinavian Americans, want to see positive images of "themselves" in American history.

Eurocentric Histories Omit the Possibility of Afro-Phoenicians

African Americans who present positive facts about African history and positive images of African Americans get accused of teaching Afrocentric history. Some white historians oppose Afrocentrism. Arthur M. Schlesinger Jr. denounced it as "psychotherapy" for blacks—a one-sided attempt to make African Americans feel good about themselves. Unfortunately, the regular history in our textbooks has been Eurocentric. So is it psychotherapy for whites?[40]

Why do textbooks leave out the possibility of the Afro-Phoenicians? Textbook authors are Eurocentric. They believe that most important developments in world history came from Europe. As Samuel Marble put it, "the possibility of African discovery of America has never been a tempting one for American historians."[41] White histo-

38. New York: Crown, 1975, 118. Archaeologist John Sorenson says, about von Wuthenau's collection, "I have studied all the written sources by Wuthenau and am confident that the figurines he illustrates are authentically ancient, at least most of them. In another publication, I reproduce a number of faces from figurines, some from von Wuthenau and others published by others, especially by Gonzalez Calderon, a physician who lives in Coatzacoalcos, Veracruz, Mexico, and who has an immense collection which he has personally gathered from La Venta and other 'Olmec' sites. These show a great variety of physical types present in ancient Mesoamerica" (e-mail, January 2014).
39. For example, "Acknowledge Your Own History" by the Jungle Brothers.
40. See Arthur Schlesinger Jr., "When Ethnic Studies Are Un-American," *Social Studies Review* 5 (Summer 1990): 11–13. A question remains: is Eurocentric or Afrocentric history *good* psychotherapy? Perhaps there are healthier therapies that don't require leaving out "the bad parts" in order to help children feel good about themselves.

rians continue to resist demands from African Americans for histories that include the accomplishments of black people. They argue that the case for the Afro-Phoenicians hasn't been proven; we mustn't distort history to improve black children's self-image. They're right in saying that the case hasn't been proven, but textbooks should include the Afro-Phoenicians as a *possibility*, a controversy. Of course, our discussion of archaeology already noted that history books aren't good at controversies. They seem to have to teach "right answers," even when no sure answer exists.

Why Do Authors Include da Gama and Not the Afro-Phoenicians?

It would be nice if some clear rule explained which events "make it" into American history textbooks. Columbus should get in: his first two voyages changed the course of human events. Authors are right to devote space to him. Textbooks also give space to people who had little effect on human events, however. They should. But *which* people? Authors' choices make a difference to readers today.

Imagine this tenth-grade classroom scene in American history. The textbook is *Life and Liberty*. It is early fall. Students are reading chapter 2, "Exploration and Colonization." An African American girl shoots up her hand to challenge the statement "not until 1497–1499 did the Portuguese explorer Vasco da Gama sail around Africa." Afrocentric rap songs are her favorite. From them she knows that Afro-Phoenicians beat da Gama by more than 2,000 years. What happens next?

Maybe the teacher takes time to research the question and learns that the student is right, the textbook wrong. Maybe s/he puts down the student's knowledge: "Rap songs aren't appropriate in a *history* class!" More likely s/he humors the girl: "Yes, but that was long ago and didn't lead to anything. Vasco da Gama's discovery is the important one." This response seems logical and allows the class to move on to the next topic. It also contains some truth. The Afro-Phoenician circumnavigation of Africa didn't lead to any new trade routes or national alliances. That's because the Africans and Phoenicians were already trading with India through the Red Sea and the Persian Gulf.

Textbooks don't include Vasco da Gama just because something came from his "discovery," however. They include him because he was white. Only one book, *The*

American People, admits this. It calls him "the first European to sail around the Cape of Africa." The rest call him the first *person*. Furthermore, all the textbooks heroify da Gama. That is, they present him in a "gee-whiz" tone that tells us he was great and we are to think well of him. As with Columbus, authors never tell what da Gama did with India, once he reached it. In fact, da Gama's journeys, like Columbus's, prove to be a mixture of heroic exploits and exploitation. Like the Spaniards, the Portuguese denied the humanity of non-Christians. To Muslims in particular, they did anything they wanted. Here is a detail from da Gama's second trip to India, in 1506, written by Gaspar Correa, a Portuguese historian who came to live in India about six years later. Da Gama's ships had just finished shelling Calicut over a disagreement with its ruler, when about twenty Moorish ships and sambuks[42] arrived at the port.

> [The Portuguese] caravels went to them, and the Moors could not fly, as they were laden, and the caravels brought them to [da Gama]. . . . He then ordered the boats to go and plunder the small vessels, which were sixteen, and the two ships, in which they found rice and many jars of butter, and many bales of stuffs. . . . Then [da Gama] commanded them to cut off the hands and ears and noses of all the crews, and put all that into one of the small vessels. . . . When all the Indians had been thus [done to], he ordered their feet to be tied together, as they had no hands with which to untie them; and in order that they should not untie them with their teeth, he ordered them to strike upon their teeth with staves, and they knocked them down their throats; and they were thus put

41. *Before Columbus*, 25.
42. A sailing ship, of the generic class dhow, with lateen sails.

on board, heaped up upon the top of each other, mixed up with the blood which streamed from them; and he ordered mats and dry leaves to be spread over them, and the sails to be set for the shore, and the vessel set on fire; and there were more than 800 Moors; and the small vessel with the friar, with all the hands and ears, was also sent on shore under sail, without being fired. These vessels went at once on shore, where many people flocked together to put out the fire, and draw out those whom they found alive, upon which they made great lamentations.[43]

No wonder the famous South African musician Hugh Masekela recorded an anticolonialist song with the refrain, "Vasco da Gama was no friend of mine."

Consider another famous explorer, Hernando de Soto. Two pages after da Gama, *Life and Liberty* tells us that de Soto "discovered [the] Mississippi River." Actually, ancestors of the Native Americans who later chased him down it had discovered and named it "Mississippi" long before. De Soto's "discovery" led to no trade, no white settlement. His was merely the first *white* face to gaze upon the Mississippi River. That's why 18 of 22 U.S. history textbooks include him. Actually, de Soto's sojourn did have one tragic result: his soldiers gave the Natives diseases that cut their population in what is now the southeastern United States to one-tenth its former number. Even by the time La Salle floated down the Mississippi 140 years later, this epidemic left Native populations much reduced. Among our 22 textbooks only *Life and Liberty* mentions this plague, and *Life and*

In this massive "historical" painting in the United States Capitol, Hernando de Soto "discovers" the Mississippi River. This stereotypical conquistador image is silly: either the Natives are freezing or the Spanish are very hot in their armor. At least the diorama does include Native bystanders, so the thoughtful viewer realizes that de Soto wasn't discovering anything. Unfortunately, archetypal images of triumphant European explorers like this affect our thinking. In reality, the Spaniards hardly looked this heroic, for the Choctaws had burned most of their clothes in an earlier battle, so the Spaniards were wearing replacements woven from reeds. De Soto had to post guards to keep his own followers from defecting to live with the Indians. A serious textbook would show the Spaniards far more bedraggled than the Natchez Indians who chased them down the Mississippi in their canoes, but no book has yet shown a bedraggled de Soto. Such an accurate portrayal of de Soto might imply that Indian societies were in some ways equal or superior to Spanish society, just as an accurate account of the defections from de Soto might suggest that Europeans found Indian societies more attractive than Indians found Europeans. (Not one Indian defected to de Soto.) Then the replacement of Indian societies by European societies might not seem such a glorious pageant of progress, in which Indians are reduced to mere predecessors or obstacles. Indian societies might appear as real alternatives.

43. Gaspar Correa, *The Three Voyages of Vasco Da Gama* (London: Hakluyt Society, 1869), 331–32.

Liberty gives it just five words. So watch out! Even after the improvements wrought by the protests and scholarship around 1992, textbooks still don't give you the whole truth.

The exploits of many explorers, from de Soto to Peary at the North Pole to the first man on the moon, didn't lead to much. Our hypothetical teacher subtly changed the ground rules for da Gama. They changed right back for de Soto. Our hypothetical tenth grader may not understand exactly what happened, but she probably senses that black feats are not considered important while white ones are. Appalling results of the explorations—a boatload of hands and ears, a devastating plague—are left out, so we can admire the courage of our white predecessors.

West Africans Versus Irish Explorers

We can explore the Eurocentrism of our textbooks if we examine what they say about some other explorers in Table 1. On purpose or by accident, people may have come to America from the west coast of Ireland around 600 A.D. and from the west coast of Africa around 1300 A.D. Let's compare the evidence for each of these voyages, then contrast what the textbooks say about them.

Moderately good evidence suggests that West Africans reached the Caribbean and Brazil in the 1300s. When Columbus reached Haiti, the Arawaks gave him some spear points made of "guanine." The Indians said they got them from black traders who came from the south and east. Guanine proved to be an alloy made of gold, silver, and copper, identical to the gold alloy preferred by West Africans, who also called it "guanine." Additional evidence comes from Islamic historians, who recorded stories of voyages west from Mali in West Africa in about 1311. From time to time in the 1300s and 1400s, shipwrecked African vessels washed up on Cape Verde, apparently from the transatlantic trade. From contacts in West Africa, the Portuguese collected considerable evidence that African traders were visiting Brazil and Central America in the mid-1400s. The first Europeans to reach Panama—Balboa and company—reported seeing black slaves in a Native town. The Indians said they captured them from a nearby black community. Oral history from Afro-Mexicans tells of pre-Columbian crossings from West Africa. In all, then, data from various sources combine to suggest that voyages from Africa probably took place, although we can't be certain.[44]

In contrast, the evidence for an Irish trip to America comes from only one side of the Atlantic. Irish legends written in the ninth or tenth century tell of "an abbot and seventeen monks who journeyed to the 'promised land of the saints.'" "The journey took place centuries earlier and lasted seven years. The account includes details that are literally fabulous. Each Easter, the priest and his crew supposedly conducted Mass on the back of a whale. They visited a "pillar of crystal" (perhaps an iceberg) and an "island of fire." We cannot simply dismiss the fable, however. Norse sagas tell us that when the Norse first reached Iceland, Irish monks were living there. Its volcanoes could have provided the "island of fire." We have no confirmation of the saga from this side of the Atlantic, however. We can only guess whether the holy men reached the Americas.[45]

How do U.S. history textbooks treat these two possible sets of voyagers? Five of them admit the possibility of St. Brendan, an Irish monk who may have crossed the Atlantic around 530 A.D. *Challenge of Freedom* gives the fullest account:

> Some people believe that . . . Irish missionaries may have sailed to the Americas hundreds of years before the first voyages of Columbus. According to Irish legends, Irish monks sailed the Atlantic Ocean in order to bring Christianity to the people they met. One Irish legend in particular tells about a land southwest of the Azores. This land was supposedly discovered by St. Brendan, an Irish missionary, about 500 A.D.

Not one book mentions West Africans, however.[46] Again, such unequal treatment smacks of Eurocentrism.

44. Van Sertima, *They Came Before Columbus*, 21, 26; regarding African diseases in the Americas, see Sorenson and Raish, *Pre-Columbian Contact with the Americas Across the Oceans*, #H344. Forbes, *Black Africans and Native Americans*, cautions that "black" or "Negro" might be misleading terms, for Europeans often applied them to any dark person of low status. Forbes does believe Balboa saw blacks but thinks they might have come somehow from Haiti. Since African slaves were brought to Haiti only in 1505, and Balboa was the first Spaniard to get to this part of Panama, they would have had to have escaped from Haiti to Panama with American Indians to precede Balboa by 1510. Regarding black oral tradition in Mexico, see Gonzalo Aguirre Beltran, *La población negra de Mexico* (Mexico City: Fondo de Cultura Económica, 1989); and John G. Jackson, *Man, God, and Civilization* (New Hyde Park, NY: University Books, 1972), 283. On nicotine and cocaine, see John Sorenson and Carl Johannesson, "Biological Evidence for Pre-Columbian Transoceanic Voyages," in *Contact and Exchange in the Ancient World*, ed. Victor Mair (Honolulu: U. of Hawaii Press, 2006), 248; and "The Curse of the Cocaine Mummies," UK Channel 4, channel4.co.uk/, September 8, 1996.
45. Cf. C.D. Riley, *Man Across the Sea*, especially Alice B. Kehoe, "Small Boats upon the North Atlantic," 275–92.

Were Columbus and the Spanish
**Were Columbus and the Spanish
Settlers or Conquerors?
8–13, 32–34**

**Explorers Before
Columbus
16–28**

**Genocide
in Haiti
37–39**

**How Long Did
It Take?
32**

**War of the Worlds
35–36**

**Making the Native
Americans Pay
35–39**

**Columbus and
Slavery
36–37, 52–53**

**Native American
Civilizations
2–5**

**"Discovering" People
Who Already Lived Here
8–13**

What the Textbooks Don't Tell You

Columbus on Haiti, A War of the Worlds

What did Columbus do with the Native Americans once he encountered them? Most histories tell us nothing.

On his first voyage, Columbus noted how the Americans "did not know what weapons are, since they neither have nor use them." He concluded, "I could conquer the whole of them with fifty men and govern them as I pleased."

On his second voyage, Columbus proceeded to do just that. In the words of Las Casas,

Since the Admiral perceived that daily the people of the land were taking up arms, ridiculous weapons in reality, and their dislike of the Christians was growing, not considering the justice and reason the Indians had for this, he hastened to proceed to the country

and disperse and subdue, by force of arms, the people of the entire island. . . . For this he chose 200 foot and 20 cavalry, with many crossbows and small cannon, lances, and swords, and a still more terrible weapon against the Indians, in addition to the horses: this was 20 hunting dogs, who were turned loose and immediately tore the Indians apart.

What the Textbooks Don't Tell You

Columbus Made the Survivors Pay

Ferdinand Columbus tells us,

[The Admiral] reduced the Indians to such obedience and tranquility that they all promised to pay tribute to the Catholic Sovereigns every three months, as follows: In the Cibao [part of Haiti], where the gold mines were, every person of 14 years of age or upward was to pay a large hawk's bell of gold dust; all others were each to pay 25 pounds of cotton. Whenever an Indian delivered his tribute, he was to receive a brass or copper token which he must wear about his neck as proof that he had made his payment. Any Indian found without such a token was to be punished.

Columbus's son fails to mention how the Spanish punished natives whose tokens had expired. They cut off their hands.

Then Columbus imposed the *encomienda* system, in which he "commended" (gave) native villages to colonists. The colonists made the Indians mine gold for them, raise Spanish crops and livestock, and even carry Spaniards whenever they wished to go somewhere. The Indians couldn't stand it. Pedro de Cordoba wrote in a letter to King Ferdinand in 1517,

As a result of the sufferings and hard labor they endured, the Indians choose and have chosen suicide. Occasionally a hundred have committed mass suicide. The women, exhausted by labor, have shunned conception and childbirth, so that work should not be heaped on them during pregnancy or after delivery. Many, when pregnant, have taken something to abort and have aborted. Others after delivery have killed their children with their own hands, so as not to leave them in such oppressive slavery.

Textbooks still don't picture Columbus's wars against the Indians. Not one mentions their suicides. Mostly they just say vague things like this, from *Pathways to the Present*: "Columbus proved to be a far better admiral than governor."

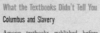

What the Textbooks Didn't Tell You

Columbus and Slavery

Among textbooks published before 1992, only two in sixteen even mentioned Columbus's enslavement of Native Americans. The rest only praised him—"a man of vision, energy, resourcefulness, and courage," in the words of *The American Pageant*. The six new books, published since 2000, are much more accurate. Two even include boxes

that give positives and negatives about Columbus and do mention his enslaving the Arawaks.

Indeed, Columbus himself started the Atlantic slave trade. He wrote to the king and queen during his second voyage:

In the name of the Holy Trinity, we can send from here all the slaves and brazilwood which could be sold. . . . In Castile, Portugal, Aragon, Italy, Sicily, and the islands of Portugal and Aragon and the Canary islands they need many slaves, and I do not think they get enough from Guinea [West Africa]. Even though they may get enough, one Indian is worth three Negroes. . . . Although they die now, they will not always die. The Negroes and Canary Islanders died at first.

Columbus sent 5,000 Indian slaves from Haiti to the Canaries and Spain. Later, others followed suit: the Portuguese shipped them from Labrador to Madeira, the British from South Carolina to Barbados, the French from Mississippi to Haiti, and the Pilgrims from Connecticut to Bermuda. But because the Indians kept dying, this slavery then led to the massive slave trade moving the other way across the Atlantic, from Africa. Columbus's son started this trade in 1505 from Guinea to Haiti. In all, about ten million Africans were sent to the Americas.

The island of Hispaniola, or Little Spain, was chosen for the first settlement and a colony was organized. Eventually, the settlers established outposts on other islands. —*The United States: A History of the Republic*

The next day at noon we saw another island [Montserrat] . . . but as the Indian women whom we brought with us said that it was not inhabited . . . we made no stay in it. . . . Another day at the dinner hour we arrived at an island [St. Martin] which seemed to be worth finding, for judging by the extent of cultivation on it, it appeared very populous. —Columbus, Letter

Columbus and the Spanish were not settlers. "Settlers" are usually families, but no women came. Settlers look for land on which to settle, but when Columbus reached Montserrat, he didn't bother to stop. No one lived there, so there was no treasure to steal. His second expedition was an armed force to subdue the Indians and take gold and other wealth from them. The "settlers" were seventeen ships of soldiers and adventurers, with cannon, guns, crossbows, horses with cavalrymen, and attack dogs in armor. Finally, Columbus decided on Hispaniola (called Haiti by the Indians, now Haiti and the Dominican Republic), because of its large Indian population and rumors that they had gold.

For thousands of years these tribal societies knew nothing of the rest of the world. They were as isolated from their original homeland in Asia and from Europe and Africa as if they were on the moon. —*American History*

To make a better myth, textbooks leave out explorers who arrived before Columbus, especially those from lands other than Europe. These included Inuits (Eskimos); perhaps Africans, Phoenicians, and Basques; and conceivably Chinese, West Africans, Indonesians, and others. This enormous stone head with possibly African features is one of over a dozen that have been found on the Atlantic coast of Mexico. They suggest that Africans and Phoenicians may have reached the Americas before 700 B.C. Contact across the Atlantic and Pacific before 1492 is a hot issue in archaeology. History texts completely skip this controversy to make Columbus "the first."

The Indians were used as a source of cheap labor for farming, ranching, and mining gold and silver. —*The American Tradition*

Forty years the Spaniards ranged those lands, massacring the wretched Indians until in Hispaniola, which in 1492 had a population estimated at 3,000,000 people, scarcely 300 Indians remained to be counted. —Las Casas

Haiti under the Spanish is one of the major genocides in all human history. Yet in 1992, only three of sixteen textbooks even mentioned the extermination of the Arawaks. But three of the six books published since 2000 treat this catastrophic population decline, produced by Spanish arms, slavery, and diseases. To replace the dying laborers, Spaniards ferried more than forty thousand Indians from the Bahamas to the gold mines of Haiti and Cuba. Packed in below deck, with hatchways closed to prevent them from escaping, a third of them died on the trip. In the words of Las Casas, "a ship without a compass, chart, or guide, but only following the trail of dead Indians who had been thrown from the ships, could find its way from the Bahamas to Hispaniola."

Christopher Col[umbus]
Indies and the Ca[...]

Then, in the presen[ce] there, he took posses[sion] Sovereigns with ap[...]
Ferdinand Colum[bus]

Textbooks say that Columbus "discovered" a "New World." But it here—they watched him "discover" it! The Americas were new only [to the peo]ple had discovered them 12,000 to 70,000 years earlier. By 1492 b[...] lived in them, about as many as in Europe. Hernán Cortés called [...] here, "larger and more pleasant" than any city in Spain.

Using "discovery" as an excuse, Columbus decreed that the lands [...] of Native Americans who spoke no Spanish, the colonists read p[...] renounce their religion and swear allegiance to Christ or else the [...] conquering them.

These possession rituals were so ridiculous that a few years ago so[me...] process around: they disembarked at the airport in Rome and procla[...]

LIES
ABO[UT]

*In 33 days I passed
Indies.* —Columb[us]

To make a better m[...] ger than it did. As [...] tual trip across the [...] Columbus had spe[nt...] repairing his ships [...]

NORTH
AMERICA

CUBA

BAHA[MAS]

SO[UTH]
AM[ERICA]

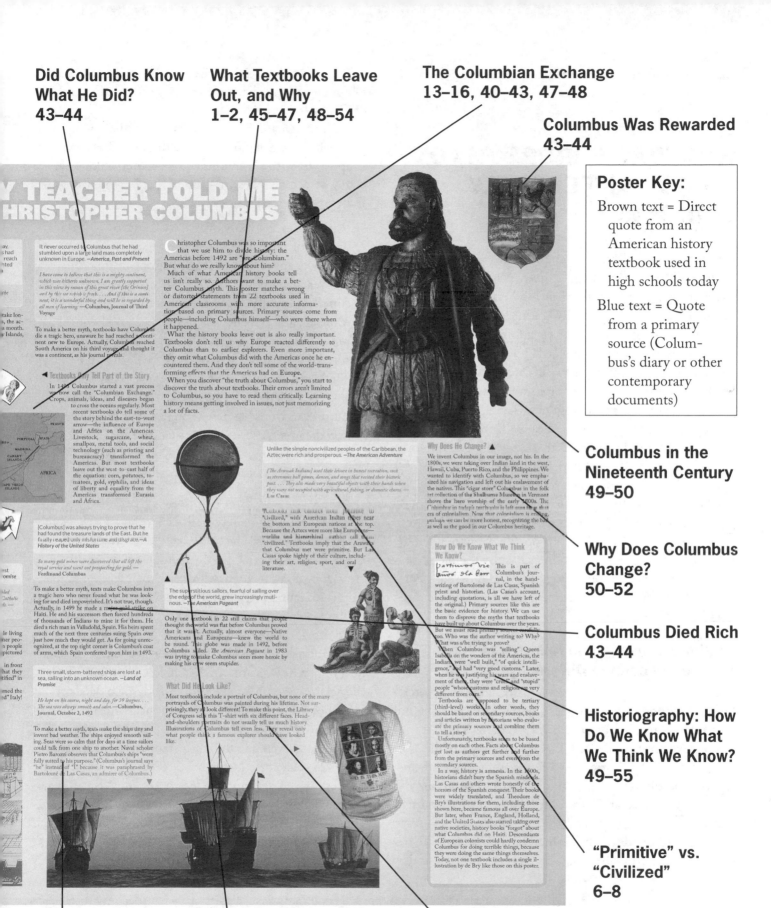

Did Columbus Know What He Did?
43–44

What Textbooks Leave Out, and Why
1–2, 45–47, 48–54

The Columbian Exchange
13–16, 40–43, 47–48

Columbus Was Rewarded
43–44

Poster Key:

Brown text = Direct quote from an American history textbook used in high schools today

Blue text = Quote from a primary source (Columbus's diary or other contemporary documents)

Columbus in the Nineteenth Century
49–50

Why Does Columbus Change?
50–52

Columbus Died Rich
43–44

Historiography: How Do We Know What We Think We Know?
49–55

"Primitive" vs. "Civilized"
6–8

Myths About the Trip
32–33

The Flat Earth Myth
15, 33–34

What Did He Look Like?
31–32

An Irish possibility merits telling. An African possibility does not.

WHY WAS EUROPE READY TO ACT DIFFERENTLY THIS TIME?

Columbus's significance owes to his *second* voyage, not his first. His first trip, in and of itself, was no more earth-shaking than that by Thorfinn and Gudrid Karlsefni in 1005. If people repeatedly journeyed to the Americas, what was different about Columbus's voyages? This question amounts to asking, what was different about Europe in 1493 compared to 1005 (or to Egypt in 700 B.C.),[47] because Columbus's importance owes to changes in Europe, not to his reaching "new" lands. The year 1493 was epoch making precisely because Europe was ready to react differently. Indeed, these same developments in Europe made it certain that Europeans soon would have reached the Americas even if Columbus had never lived. For that matter, they may already have done so. A 1497 letter by a Bristol (England) businessman states, "the cape of the said land [probably Newfoundland] was found and discovered in times past by the men from Bristol." This letter implies that British and perhaps Portuguese fishermen were already fishing off Newfoundland before 1492.[48]

Textbooks Give Vague Answers to Why Europe Responded Differently

We have seen that textbooks mostly ignore explorers before Columbus. Nevertheless, authors do understand that Columbus's importance owes to changes in Europe. Some texts even point out that history passed the Vikings by because Europe "was not ready to take advantage of the discovery," as one puts it. American history books devote several pages to developments that caused Europe to be "ready" this time.

Most authors do note the increase of trade and merchants. Some describe the rise of nation-states under kings and queens. Otherwise, though, they do an awful job telling of the changes in Europe that led to the Age of Conquest.

All but two of 22 textbooks begin their Columbus story with Marco Polo and the Crusades. (The other two simply start with Columbus.) Here is their composite account of the changes in Europe. Each sentence comes from an American history book.

"Life in Europe was slow paced." "Curiosity about the rest of the world was at a low point." Then, "Many changes took place in Europe during the 500 years before Columbus's discovery of the Americas in 1492." "People's horizons gradually widened, and they became more curious about the world beyond their own localities." "Europe was stirring with new ideas. Many Europeans were filled with burning curiosity. They were living in a period called the Renaissance." "What started Europeans thinking new thoughts and dreaming new dreams? A series of wars called the Crusades were partly responsible." "The Crusades caused great changes in the ways that Europeans thought and acted."

Different accounts resemble each other closely. Sometimes they even use the same words. However, although these sketches of changes in Europe are extensive, they are vague and unfocused. Moreover, their level of scholarship is discouragingly low. Probably, authors are more at home in American history than European history. They don't provide causal explanations for the Age of European Conquest. Instead, they argue for Europe's greatness in psychological terms. "People grew more curious," they claim. Arguments like that make sociologists smile. We know that nobody measured the curiosity level in Spain in 1492, compared to Norway or Iceland in 1005. Some books even cite the Protestant Reformation, but it began 25 years *after* 1492!

Here is the account in *The Americans*: "The Renaissance encouraged people to regard themselves as individuals, to have confidence in human capabilities, and to look forward to the fame their achievements might bring. This attitude prompted many to seek glory

---

46. *A History of the Republic* does devote part of a sentence to the "claim that Africans explored parts of the Americas several hundred years before Columbus," but seems to be referring to the Afro-Phoenicians rather than West Africans. In any case, this text dismisses their likelihood and importance: "None of these Europeans, Africans, or Asians left lasting traces of their presence in the Americas, nor did they develop any lasting relationships with the first Americans."
47. Some of the other possible explorers listed in Table 1 might have made round-trips. Some of them might have led to additional voyages. We don't know.
48. David Quinn, *England and the Discovery of America*, 5–105; see also Robert Blow, *Abroad in America* (New York: Continuum, 1990), 17; Forbes, *Black Africans and Native Americans*, 20; and Crone, *Discovery of America*, 156–59.

through adventure, discovery, and conquest." Now Europeans had "confidence in human capabilities." Pretty vague!

The Topic—Why Was Europe Able to Dominate the World?—Is Crucial

What is going on here? We must pay attention to what authors are telling us and what they are not telling us. The topic could hardly be more significant. The changes in Europe didn't just prompt Columbus's 1492 voyage and the probable trips to America at about the same time by Portuguese, Basque, and Bristol fishermen. They also led to Columbus's 1493 voyage and then to Europe's control of the world. From 1450 to about 1950, European and European-derived nations, including the United States, Canada, and Australia, dominated the world. In some ways, they still do. Except for the invention of agriculture, this was probably the most important development in human history. Our history textbooks ought to discuss seriously why it happened.

Here is what the books leave out.

Europe Had Developed New Military Technology, Social Technology, Religious Thought, and Experience in Colonialism

We have seen that cultures usually develop through syncretism—combining ideas from other societies to form something new. Trade with Arabs in the Mediterranean and to the east indeed brought new ideas to Europe. Military technology was the most important single development. Europeans learned about gunpowder and cannons in 1241 from Mongols who were attacking from the east. Beginning about 1400, European rulers ordered bigger and bigger guns and learned to mount them on ships. Europe's incessant wars gave rise to this arms race, which also included developments in archery, drill, and siege warfare. China, the Ottoman Empire (now roughly Turkey), and other nations in Asia and Africa now fell prey to European arms. Beginning in 1493, the Americas succumbed. We live with this arms race today. Western nations still try with some success to keep non-Western nations disadvantaged in arms.[49] Nonetheless, only one textbook mentions arms as a cause of European world domination.

> ### Doing History: Understanding Syncretism
> Explain Christmas, gumbo, and jazz as examples of syncretism.

Cannons and caravels weren't the only new things Europeans had going for them. Europe also expanded the use of new forms of social technology—bureaucracy, double-entry bookkeeping, literacy, and printing. "Bureaucracy" is a negative word today, but actually it was a practical development that allowed rulers and merchants to manage far-flung enterprises efficiently. So did double-entry bookkeeping, based on the decimal system, which Europeans had learned from Arab traders. Literacy and the printing press allowed news of Columbus's findings to travel across Europe much farther and faster than news of the Vikings'.

A third change in Europe was in how people thought about money. Many societies don't value wealth. To them it implies selfishness. Christianity reflected this view in Christ's teaching, "It is easier for a camel to pass through a needle's eye than for a rich man to enter heaven." Christianity was changing in Europe, however. Amassing wealth and dominating other people were becoming key ways to win status. As Columbus put it, "Gold is most excellent; gold constitutes treasure; and he who has it does all he wants in the world, and can even lift souls up to Paradise." In 1005 the Vikings intended only to settle "Vineland." By 1493 the Spaniards planned to plunder Haiti.[50]

Another development was Europeans' recent success in taking over and exploiting or exterminating other island societies. On Malta, Sardinia, and the Canary Islands, Europeans had learned that this was a route to wealth. Later the British did the same in Ireland. In *Columbus, His Enterprise*, novelist Hans Koning characterizes Europe in biting words: "What sets the West apart is its persistence, its capacity to *stop at nothing*."[51] He has a point: consider da Gama's actions at Kolkata, for example.

---

49. William H. McNeill, *The Age of Gunpowder Empires* (Washington: American Historical Association, 1989). Arms control for non-Europeans has been a theme throughout American history. The thirteen British colonies tried to keep Native Americans from getting guns. Today the United States tries to keep countries such as Iran and North Korea from getting nuclear weapons.
50. Letter to the king and queen of Spain, July 1503, quoted in Salvador de Madariaga, *Christopher Columbus* (New York: Frederick Ungar, 1967 [1940]), 379, and in *Select Letters of Christopher Columbus*, trans. and ed. R.H. Major (New York: Corinth, 1961 [1847]), 196.
51. New York: Monthly Review Press, 1976, 122 (his italics).

Finally, new and more deadly forms of smallpox and bubonic plague had arisen in Europe since the Vikings sailed. We have seen how they helped Europe conquer.[52]

Textbooks Omit the Causes of Conquest

Except for the printing press, no text mentions any of these causes.

Why don't authors mention arms as a cause of exploration and domination? Why don't they tell us of Europe's prior experiments with colonization on Malta and the Canaries? Because those topics aren't nice? Because they reflect badly on us? Certainly such factors are less endearing than "the Renaissance," "curiosity about the world," or "humanism," which authors do supply as causes of European conquest.

If nasty causes like military power or religiously approved greed reflect badly on us, who exactly is "us"? Who are the books written for (and by)? Plainly, descendants of the Europeans, not people of color. Texts seem to want to avoid offending "us" by not telling any bad things Europeans did or any awkward factors that lay behind their (our?) deeds. Thus omitting the cruder causes of European expansion might be termed a whitewash.

The Whitewash Hinders Us from Thinking Intelligently About the Question

My college students rarely thought in high school about why Europe rose to world domination. It's not usually presented as a question; it seems natural, a given, even rather nice, not something to be explained. Deep down, our culture encourages us to imagine it's because we're smarter. Of course, we know better than to believe that. We know that no studies show Americans to be more intelligent than, say, Iraqis. Still, textbooks don't encourage us to think about the real causes, so "we're smarter" hangs around as a possibility.

Take a Position: Why Did Europe Win?

What were the most important causes that enabled Europeans to conquer Haiti and the Americas? Which of these factors have relevance today? What relevance?

The way U.S. history textbooks treat Columbus reinforces this tendency not to think about it. This is unfortunate, because Columbus's voyages provide a splendid teachable moment. They exemplify the new Europe, being official missions of a nation-state. Merchants and rulers combined to finance and authorize them. The second expedition was heavily armed. Columbus carefully documented the voyages. Gutenberg had invented the printing press, so detailed news of Haiti and later landfalls spread swiftly. Columbus had personal experience with the Atlantic islands recently subjugated by Portugal and Spain and with the slave trade on West Africa. Most important, his purpose from the beginning was not mere exploration or even trade. It was conquest and exploitation, for which he used religion openly as a rationale.[53] If textbooks included these facts, they might induce students to think intelligently about why the West dominates the world today.

Textbooks Are Wrong About Muslims

Related to the changes in Europe is the question: what caused Europe to turn west in search of the East? Textbooks used to claim that Europe needed spices to cover up the taste of bad meat. Then the Turks cut off the spice trade. Three books in my sample, written before 1992, still claimed that the Turks forced Europe into seeking new routes to China. Historian A.H. Lybyer disproved this error in 1915! Turkey had nothing to do with the development of new routes to the Indies. On the contrary, the Turks had every reason to keep the old eastern Mediterranean route open, since they made money from it.[54]

Thankfully, none of the new books makes this error. Lamentably, some teachers, having learned it wrong when they were in school, still teach it. Probably textbooks should take time to teach *against* the myth, because otherwise it will stay alive in our culture. That's because blaming Turkey fits with the West's unstated assumption that followers of Islam are likely to behave irrationally. This kind of argument makes Christians the good guys, Muslims the bad guys. Columbus becomes the first good guy. Congressman Roland Libonati, the leader favoring Columbus Day when Congress was making it a holiday in 1963, put it this way: "His Christian faith gave to him a religious incentive to thwart the piratical activities of the Turkish marauders preying upon the trading ships

---

52. See Alfred Crosby, *Ecological Imperialism*, 71–93.
53. Sale, *Conquest of Paradise*, 71–72. In *Spanish Main* (23, 34), Sauer suggests religion was a mere rationale for Columbus.
54. A.H. Lybyer, "The Ottoman Turks and the Routes of Oriental Trade," *English Historical Review 30*, no. 120 (October 1915): 577–88. Turkey may have shut out Portuguese and Spanish merchants from the trade for a time, however, owing to warfare between Turkey and Spain/Portugal.

of the Christian world." But it never happened that way. We saw how Vasco da Gama acted as a pirate in 1506 in Kolkata. The next year the Portuguese fleet blocked the Red Sea and Persian Gulf to stop the trade along the old route. Why? Because they controlled the new one, around Africa, and wanted to corner the market.

Errors like this teach us to read more critically. Often when we look closely at what textbooks say, they're wrong.

TEXTBOOKS MAKE UP DETAILS ABOUT COLUMBUS TO AVOID UNCERTAINTY

When they reach the Columbus story itself, authors continue to make mistakes. They present cut-and-dried answers, avoiding uncertainty or controversy. They glorify Columbus. Often their errors seem to be copied from other textbooks.

Let me repeat the collective Columbus story, told by American history books, with which this book began. This time I will italicize everything in it that we have solid reason to believe is true.

> *Born* in Genoa, of humble parents, *Christopher Columbus grew up to become an experienced seafarer, venturing as far as Iceland and West Africa.* His experiences convinced him that the world must be round and that the fabled riches of the East— spices and gold—could be had by sailing west, replacing the overland routes which the Turks had closed off to commerce. *To get funding for his enterprise, he beseeched monarch after monarch in Western Europe.* Finally, after being dismissed once more by Ferdinand and Isabella of Spain, Columbus got his chance. *Isabella decided to underwrite a* modest *expedition. He outfitted three* pitifully small *ships, Niña, Pinta, and Santa María, and set forth from Spain. After* an arduous *journey* of more than two months, during which his mutinous crew almost threw him overboard, he discovered the *West Indies on October 12, 1492.* Unfortunately, although *he made three more voyages to America*, he never knew he had discovered a New World. *Columbus died* in obscurity,

Most textbooks include a portrait of Columbus, but we don't even know what he looked like. Not one of the many portrayals of Columbus was painted during his lifetime. Not surprisingly, they all look different! To make this point, the Library of Congress sold this T-shirt with six different faces.

Head-and-shoulders portraits do not usually tell us much history anyway, unless you believe you can read character from eye set. Illustrations of Columbus tell even less. They reveal only what people think a famous explorer *should* have looked like.

unappreciated and penniless. Nevertheless, without his daring, *American history would have been* very *different*, for in a sense he made it all possible.

As you can see, textbooks get the date right and the names of the ships. Most of the rest that they tell us is untrustworthy.

We Aren't Sure of His Background

Many aspects of Columbus's life remain a mystery. Historians are not certain of his background. He claimed to be from Genoa, Italy, and there is evidence that he was. But there is also evidence that he wasn't: he didn't seem to be able to write in Italian, even when writing to people in Genoa. Some historians believe he was Jewish, a *converso*, that is, a Jewish convert to Christianity, probably from Spain. (Spain was pressuring its Jews to convert to Christianity or leave the country.) He may have been of Jewish background in Genoa. Still other historians claim he was from Corsica, Portugal, or somewhere else.[55]

If we're not certain as to his geographic origin, what about his social class background? We don't know. But

---

55. The three small fragments of knowledge about Columbus's background are described in Lorenzo Camusso, *The Voyages of Columbus* (New York: Dorset, 1991), 9–10. See also Sale, *Conquest of Paradise*, 51–52.

The American People knows he was poor—"the son of a poor Genoese weaver"—while Boorstin and Kelley know he was rich—"the son of a prosperous wool-weaver." Authors are certain about facts that people who have spent years studying Columbus say we cannot be sure of!

Textbooks Tell Falsehoods About Columbus's First Voyage

It's scary how books sometimes disagree. What was the weather like during Columbus's 1492 trip? According to *Land of Promise*, his ships were "storm-battered," but Boorstin and Kelley say they enjoyed "good weather and clear sailing." How long was the voyage? "On the seventieth day, long after Columbus had calculated he would reach Japan, a lookout sighted land," according to *The American People*, but *America Past and Present* says, "the tiny Spanish fleet sighted an island in the Bahamas after only thirty-three days at sea." How were Native Americans distributed when he arrived? "Heavily populated" in *The American People*; "spread thin" in Boorstin and Kelley.

It's even scarier how texts agree! Do we know where Columbus thought he was going? Every single textbook says he was trying to reach Japan and the East Indies. Boorstin and Kelley even claim that he sailed southwest to the Canary Islands partly because "the Canaries were on the same latitude as Japan, so if he went due west he thought he would arrive where he wanted to be."[56] Actually historians don't know whether Columbus thought he was going to Japan or was trying to reach "new" lands. Some historians point out that Columbus probably knew of the Americas. People in western Europe had imagined or heard vaguely of islands or continents to the west. Columbus had visited West Africa and probably Iceland. Voyagers from these two lands had probably reached the Americas in years past. Evidence of the Americas, even including dead American Indians, sometimes washed up on Madeira and the Azores, where Columbus had spent much of his life.[57] Moreover, he took care to negotiate an agreement with the queen and king of Spain that made him "Viceroy and Governor General in all the said islands and mainlands and in the islands which, as aforesaid, he may discover or acquire in the said seas." This agreement seems to imply that Columbus expected to reach new lands, hitherto unknown to Europe, not China and Japan. As historian Edward Bourne wrote in 1906, "It is a remarkable fact that nothing is said in this patent of discovering a route to the Indies. It is often said that the sole purpose of Columbus was to discover such a route, yet it is clear that he expected to make some new discoveries, and that if he did not, the sovereigns were under no specified obligations to him."[58] On the other hand, Columbus himself claimed to be seeking the East by sailing west. Repeatedly, he said he was near Japan or China.

Historians have asserted each viewpoint for centuries. After reviewing the evidence, a Columbus biographer, Kirkpatrick Sale, concluded, "We will likely never know for sure." Sale also noted that such a conclusion is "not very satisfactory for those who demand certainty in their historical tales."[59] All our textbooks are of this type. Authors seem compelled to give answers even when no solid answers are available. Every author "knows" he was seeking Japan. Thus, they keep their readers from realizing that historians *don't* know all the answers, so history *cannot* be just a process of memorizing them.

TEXTBOOKS MAKE THE OBSTACLES SEEM GREATER

Not all the errors textbooks make about Columbus result from sloppy scholarship. Authors are telling us a story. They want to magnify him as a great hero. Every one of them tries to get us to root for him. Authors add detail after detail to heighten our appreciation of Columbus's daring and worthiness. Here is part of the treatment in *Land of Promise*:

> It is October, 1492. Three small, storm-battered ships are lost at sea, sailing into an unknown ocean. A frightened crew has been threatening to throw their stubborn captain overboard, turn the ships around, and make for the safety of familiar shores.
>
> Then a miracle: The sailors see some green branches floating on the water. Land birds fly overhead. From high in the ship's rigging the lookout cries, "Land, land ahead!" Fears turn to joy. Soon

---

56. Palos, the Spanish port from which Columbus left, is on the same latitude as Honshu, Japan's largest island. The Canaries lie well south of Japan. In fact, Columbus went to the Canaries to repair *Pinta*'s rudder, take on more drinking water, and buy last-minute provisions. He also kindled a romance with a beautiful rich young widow there.

57. Forbes, *Black Africans and Native Americans*.

58. Edward G. Bourne, *The Northmen, Columbus, and Cabot, 985–1503* (New York: Scribner's, 1906), 77–78.

59. *Conquest of Paradise*, 23–26. See also Sauer, *Spanish Main*, 15–16.

This reenactment, photographed for *National Geographic*, accurately shows the competent ships and fair weather that marked Columbus's journey to America. (Two major storms did threaten the return trip.)

the grateful captain wades ashore and gives thanks to God.

Now, really. *Niña*, *Pinta*, and *Santa María* were not "storm-battered." To make a better myth, these authors want the trip to seem harder than it was, so they invent bad weather. Columbus's journal tells that the three ships enjoyed lovely sailing. Seas were so calm that for days at a time, sailors were able to talk from one ship to another. The only day they experienced even moderately high seas was the last, when they knew they were near land.

To make a better myth, textbooks make the ships tiny and inefficient. "Cockleshell craft," *Pageant* calls them. Actually, bigger is not necessarily safer or more efficient. "These three vessels were fully suited to his purpose," according to naval author Pietro Barozzi.

Columbus Was Smart; the Rest Were Fools

To make a better myth, to make the trip seem harder than it was, 12 of 22 textbooks magnify his crew's complaints into a near mutiny, "threatening to throw their stubborn captain overboard," in the words of *Land of Promise*. The texts exaggerate. Some primary sources claim the sailors did threaten to go back home if they didn't reach land soon. Other primary sources claim that Columbus lost heart and the captains of the other two ships persuaded him to keep on. Still other sources suggest that the leaders simply met and agreed to go on for a few more days and then reconsider the situation. Columbus biographer Samuel Eliot Morison reduced the complaints to mere griping: "They were all getting on each other's nerves, as

happens even nowadays." So much for the threat of being thrown overboard.

Why do so many authors swallow the near-mutiny story? Maybe because it fits in with their story line about how great Columbus was—how he triumphed over every adversary, even his own sorry crew. High school history teacher Bill Bigelow points out, "The sailors are stupid, superstitious, cowardly, and sometimes scheming. Columbus, on the other hand, is brave, wise, and godly." These textbook portrayals amount to an "anti–working class, pro-boss polemic," Bigelow concludes. It fits into our popular culture, which demeans the intelligence of people who work with their hands.

We have already mentioned another piece of this myth: Columbus's entering false entries in the ship's log. Columbus biographer Salvador de Madariaga points out that to believe this, we have to believe the crew members were fools. Columbus had "no special method, available only to him, whereby distances sailed could be more accurately reckoned than by the other pilots and masters." Indeed, Columbus was *less* experienced as a pilot than the Pinzón brothers, who captained *Niña* and *Pinta*.[60]

During the return voyage, Columbus confided in his journal his reason for the false log entries. He wanted to keep the route to the Indies secret. As paraphrased by Las Casas, "He says that he pretended to have gone a greater distance in order to confound the pilots and sailors who did the charts, that he might remain master of that route to the Indies."

In 1828 the World Became Flat!

In 1983 *The American Pageant* provided still another piece of this legend of a crew of fools: "The superstitious sailors, fearful of sailing over the edge of the world, grew increasingly mutinous."[61] This is nonsense. Almost no one

60. *Christopher Columbus*, 203–4.
61. *Pageant*'s authors did correct this error by 2006; now the book merely says, "His superstitious sailors, fearful of venturing into the oceanic unknown, grew increasingly mutinous." But this too is not correct, as this page has shown. Nor does it challenge the flat-earth myth in our culture.

This globe was made in Europe in 1492, *before Columbus returned.*

thought the world was flat. Most Europeans knew it was round. On this side of the Atlantic, most Native Americans saw it that way too. It *looks* round. Sailors see its roundness when ships disappear over the horizon, hull first, then sails. Columbus never had to contend with a superstitious crew worried about falling off the edge of the earth.[62]

American novelist Washington Irving, who invented Rip Van Winkle, popularized the flat-earth fable in 1828. He probably thought it added a nice dramatic flourish to his Columbus biography and would do no harm—but it did and still does. It invites us to believe that the "primitives" of the world had only a crude understanding of the planet they lived on, until a forward-thinking European man of science brought them out of darkness. Such a story line exalts Columbus's voyages from mere passages for plunder into scientific expeditions. Back in 1963, arguing for Columbus Day, Congressman Peter Rodino fell for this fable. He lauded Columbus as "a scientist, whose achievements urge us forward, on the never-ending quest for knowledge."

To their credit, only one textbook in 22 claims that people before Columbus thought the world was flat. Nevertheless, many Americans still believe this myth. Some teachers, even in the twenty-first century, still teach it. So does American culture. A character in *Star Trek V*, for instance, a movie made in 1989, repeats the Washington Irving lie: "The people of your world once believed the earth to be flat; Columbus proved it was round."

Without a doubt, Christopher Columbus was a great man. Even before he sailed to America, he had traveled as far north (Iceland), south (Guinea in West Africa), east (Turkey), and west (the Canary Islands) as anyone in Europe. In 1492 he set forth to reach a goal, enlisted the support of others, took a grand risk by venturing forth past the Canary Islands, and succeeded. Moreover, he promoted and carried out national voyages and publicized his finds. After Columbus, there would be other European explorers in the Americas who would "discover" its details, but because of Columbus America now stayed in contact with Europe. Textbooks shouldn't have to exaggerate the difficulties he overcame. His story is important enough on its own.

C. Columbus solicits funds for a promising project. Spain, 1489.

Without project funding, the world might still be flat.

Every October advertisers recycle the flat-earth theme. This ad seeks investors for daring, courageous stockbrokers!

TEXTBOOKS PURIFY HIS MOTIVES

Just as authors exaggerate the obstacles Columbus faced, they also distort his reasons for choosing to face them.

62. J.B. Russell, *Inventing the Flat Earth* (New York: Praeger, 1991).

Bill Bigelow remembers that when he was in fourth grade, the reason seemed to be "just because—because he was curious, because he loved adventure, because he wanted to prove he could do it—just because."[63] Textbooks haven't changed much since then. *American History* quotes "a doctor who knew Columbus" and "wrote that Columbus had a 'noble and grand desire to go to the places where the spices grow.'"

The truth of the matter is, Columbus was after money. So were the Spaniards who accompanied him. Columbus tells us so himself, in the journal of his first voyage, just three days after making his famous landfall on October 12, 1492: "I do not wish to delay but to discover and go to many islands to find gold."

Columbus was no greedier than the Spanish or, later, the English and French. "The search for gold was one of the main reasons for Columbus's journey," *The Americans* states plainly. For some reason, most other books downplay getting rich as a motive for coming to the Americas—not only about Columbus, but also when they describe other explorers and colonists. Even the Pilgrims were motivated primarily by money, but you'd never know it from our histories. Textbooks stress almost anything else—religion, science, curiosity, even "humanism." Authors must believe that to have America explored and colonized for greedy reasons is somehow undignified.

We have seen that a change in how people thought about money is one of the factors that now made Europe different. (The others I've discussed include guns, the rise of nation-states, social technology, new diseases, and recent experience in colonialism.) These differences set Columbus's voyages apart from all previous voyages to the Americas. Columbus valued everyone and everything according to their ability to help him find gold. He was so intent on finding riches that he transformed the Americas in the process.

Columbus's Attitude Toward the American Indians

Columbus's initial impression of the Arawaks who inhabited most of the islands in the Caribbean was quite favorable. He wrote in his journal on October 13, 1492:

> At daybreak great multitudes of men came to the shore, all young and of fine shapes, and very handsome. Their hair was not curly but loose and coarse like horse-hair. All have foreheads much broader

than any people I had hitherto seen. Their eyes are large and very beautiful. They are not black, but the color of the inhabitants of the Canaries.

This reference to the Canaries was ominous, however. Spain was then in the process of exterminating the last of the aboriginal people of those islands.

Columbus went on to describe the Arawaks' canoes, "some large enough to contain 40 or 45 men." Then he got down to business:

> I was very attentive to them, and strove to learn if they had any gold. Seeing some of them with little bits of metal hanging at their noses, I gathered from them by signs that by going southward or steering round the island in that direction, there would be found a king who possessed great cups full of gold.

TEXTBOOKS OMIT WHAT COLUMBUS DID WITH THE AMERICAS

At dawn the next day, Columbus sailed to the other shore of the island and saw two or three more villages. "They did not know what weapons are," he reported. "They neither have nor use them." He ended his description with these menacing words: "I could conquer the whole of them with fifty men and govern them as I pleased."

War of the Worlds

Columbus returned to Spain at just the right time. In 1492, Ferdinand and Isabella had just finished driving the Muslims from Granada, unifying Spain. Their large army now had nothing to do, so the rulers provided Columbus with 1,200 to 1,500 men, seventeen ships, cannons, crossbows, guns, cavalry, and attack dogs for a second voyage. One way to visualize their confrontation with the Arawaks on Haiti is with the help of the famous science-fiction book, movie, and radio show *War of the Worlds*. H.G. Wells intended his account of earthlings' terrifying encounter with technologically advanced aliens as an allegory. It represents the meeting of "primitive" peoples with technologically advanced Europeans. In the book and movie, we identify with

---

63. Bill Bigelow, "Once Upon a Genocide . . . ," in *Rethinking Columbus* (Milwaukee: Rethinking Schools, 1991), 23–30.

the helpless British. In Orson Welles's famous radio adaptation, the story is set in New Jersey and we identify with the helpless Americans. Meanwhile, Wells invites us to identify with the natives on Haiti in 1493, or the Canaries in 1450, or Australia in 1788, or the Amazon jungle today.[64]

When Columbus and his men returned to Haiti in 1493, they demanded food, gold, spun cotton—whatever the Natives had that the Spaniards wanted, including sex with their women. To ensure cooperation, Columbus used exemplary punishment. When a Native committed even a minor offense, he had the Spanish cut off the Indian's ears or nose. Then he sent the person, disfigured, back to his village as a warning.

After a while, the Arawaks had had enough. At first their resistance was mostly passive. They refused to plant food for the Spanish to take. They abandoned towns near the Spanish settlements. Finally, the Arawaks fought back. Their sticks and stones made no more impact against the armed and clothed Spanish, however, than earthlings' rifles against aliens' death rays in *War of the Worlds*.

However, the Arawaks' resistance gave Columbus an excuse to make war on them. On March 24, 1495, he set out to conquer them. Bartolomé de Las Casas tells of the force Columbus assembled to put down the rebellion.

> Since the Admiral perceived that daily the people of the land were taking up arms, ridiculous weapons in reality . . . he hastened to proceed to the country and disperse and subdue, by force of arms, the people of the entire island. . . . For this he chose 200 foot soldiers and 20 cavalry, with many crossbows and small cannon, lances, and swords, and a still more terrible weapon against the Indians, in addition to the horses: this was 20 hunting dogs, who were turned loose and immediately tore the Indians apart.[65]

Naturally, the Spanish won. According to biographer Kirkpatrick Sale, quoting from Ferdinand Columbus's biography of his father:

> The soldiers mowed down dozens with point-blank volleys, loosed the dogs to rip open limbs and bellies, chased fleeing Indians into the bush to skewer

The attack dogs were "a still more terrible weapon against the Indians" than the cannons and cavalry, in the words of Las Casas. They "tore the Indians apart." Theodore de Bry published this engraving of the scene in 1590.

them on sword and pike, and "with God's aid soon gained a complete victory, killing many Indians and capturing others who were also killed."

The war dragged on for ten months, but its outcome was never in doubt. Now Columbus ruled by terror. He set up the rule that for each Spaniard the Natives slew, the Spanish would kill a hundred Natives. (Germans used a similar rule to demoralize resistance in conquered Europe during World War II.) Afterward, Columbus set up a tribute system. Ferdinand Columbus tells how it worked:

> [The American Indians] all promised to pay tribute to the Catholic Sovereigns every three months, as follows: In the Cibao, where the gold mines were, every person of 14 years of age or upward was to pay a large hawk's bell of gold dust; all others were each to pay 25 pounds of cotton. Whenever an Indian delivered his tribute, he was to receive a brass or copper token which he must wear about his neck as proof that he had made his payment. Any Indian found without such a token was to be punished.[66]

Columbus's son fails to mention how the Spanish punished people whose tokens had expired. They cut off their hands.

Columbus Begins the Slave Trade

After the first major defeat of the Indians, Columbus

64. Philip Klass, "Wells, Welles, and the Martians," *New York Times Book Review*, October 30, 1988.
65. Quoted in Michael Paiewonsky, *The Conquest of Eden, 1493–1515* (Chicago: Academy, 1991), 109, translation modified by me based on translation in Juan Friede and Benjamin Keen, *Bartolomé de las Casas in History* (De Kalb: Northern Illinois Press, 1971), 312.
66. Ferdinand Columbus, *The Life of the Admiral Christopher Columbus* (New Brunswick: Rutgers U. Press, 1959), 149–50.

The artist Theodore de Bry never left Europe. Instead, he patterned his illustrations after the writings of Spanish historians. This one shows Spaniards cutting off American Indians' hands.

"There now began a reign of terror in Hispaniola," in the words of Hans Koning. Spaniards hunted Natives for sport and murdered them for dog food. The tribute system broke down because what it demanded was simply impossible. To replace it Columbus installed the *encomienda* system, in which he granted or "commended" American Indian villages to various colonists. Since it wasn't called slavery, this forced-labor system escaped the moral criticism that slavery received. Following Columbus's example, Spain made it official policy, and other conquistadores then brought the system to Mexico, Peru, and Florida.[68]

had his men round up 1,500 Arawaks. He then picked the 500 best specimens to send back to Spain as slaves. Two hundred died en route. Another 500 were chosen as slaves by Spaniards staying on Haiti. Columbus released the rest. A Spanish eyewitness described the panic that followed.

> Among them were many women who had infants at the breast. They, in order the better to escape us, since they were afraid we would turn to catch them again, left their infants anywhere on the ground and started to flee like desperate people; and some fled so far that they were removed from our settlement of Isabela 7 or 8 days beyond mountains.

This was the first of many large shipments that Columbus proposed. He wrote to Ferdinand and Isabella:

> In the name of the Holy Trinity, we can send from here all the slaves and brazil-wood which could be sold. . . . In Castile, Portugal, Aragon, . . . and the Canary Islands they need many slaves, and I do not think they get enough from Guinea. Even though they may get enough, one Indian is worth three Negroes. . . . Although they die now, they will not always die. The Negroes and Canary Islanders died at first.[67]

However, Queen Isabella opposed slavery, though inconsistently, and she ordered one shipment of enslaved American Indians returned to the Americas. Nevertheless, Columbus continued to enslave Indians and send them across the Atlantic.

Haiti's Native Population Is Reduced to Nothing

On Haiti the colonists made the Natives mine gold for them, raise Spanish food, and even carry them everywhere they went. The Natives couldn't stand it. Pedro de Cordoba wrote in a letter to King Ferdinand in 1517,

> As a result of the sufferings and hard labor they endured, the Indians choose and have chosen suicide. Occasionally a hundred have committed mass suicide. The women, exhausted by labor, have shunned conception and childbirth. . . . Many, when pregnant, have taken something to abort and have aborted. Others after delivery have killed their

Not one textbook mentions American Indian suicides (although *The Americans* does quote Hans Koning on "genocidal cruelty"). De Bry probably designed this engraving after de Cordoba's letter and other accounts of Natives who impaled themselves, drank poison, jumped off cliffs, hanged themselves, and killed their children. The artist decided to combine all of these methods in one picture!

67. Letter of 1496, quoted in Eric Williams, *Documents of West Indian History* (Port-of-Spain, Trinidad: PNM, 1963), 1:57.
68. The tribute, slavery, and *encomienda* systems established by Columbus are treated in Sale, *Conquest of Paradise*, 138–66; Maria Norlander-Martinez, "Christopher Columbus: The Man, the Myth, and the Slave Trade," *Adventures of the Incredible Librarian* (April 1990), 17; Las Casas, *History of the Indies* (New York: Harper and Row, 1971), 79–147; and Koning, *Columbus: His Enterprise* (New York: Monthly Review Press, 1976). John and Jeanette Varner discuss dog food in *Dogs of the Conquest* (Norman: U. of Oklahoma Press, 1983), 13.

children with their own hands, so as not to leave them in such oppressive slavery.[69]

Diseases new to the American Indians played a big role in this annihilation. Smallpox, however, usually the big killer of Natives, did not appear on the island until after 1516. But the tribute and *encomienda* systems themselves caused much of the depopulation. The Spanish forced Indians to work in the gold mines rather than in their gardens, which led to massive malnutrition. Demoralized by the conditions of forced labor, hopeless parents killed their babies and themselves. Others fled to Cuba, where they found temporary respite, but only until the Spanish arrived there. Before Columbus, more than three million people lived on Haiti. Twenty-five years after he arrived, only 12,000 remained. By 1535 fewer than 500 Arawaks survived on Haiti. By 1555, all were gone.

Textbooks Used to Whitewash Columbus

Haiti under the Spanish is one of the major cases of genocide in all human history.[70] Yet, as of 1992, textbooks omitted nasty facts like cutting off hands, replacing them instead with nice touches like "Land ahead!" Among the fifteen textbooks published before 1992, only two even mentioned the extermination of the Arawaks. But three of the six newer books treat this catastrophic population decline, and *Holt* mentions Columbus's role in it.

Only seven of fifteen histories published before 1992 told that the Spanish enslaved or exploited the Natives anywhere in the Americas, and only two implied that Columbus started it. One more admitted, "he was not good at politics or business," but that hardly says anything about slavery. Twelve said nothing about what Columbus did to the Natives once he encountered them. To magnify Columbus as hero, they left out any unpleasantness.

After 2000, most textbooks grew more honest. All but the antique Boorstin and Kelley at least mention that the Spanish enslaved American Indians. *The Americans* and *Holt* give equal space to "traditional historians" who view Columbus "as a hero" and "other historians" who stress the "fatal consequences" of his journeys. Giving both

viewpoints marks a real advance over bland treatments like this, in *Pathways*: "Columbus proved to be a far better admiral than governor."[71] Again, what happened in 1992 made a difference.

The American Indian Slave Trade Leads to the African Slave Trade

Columbus not only sent the first slaves across the Atlantic, he sent more—about 5,000—than any other individual, mostly to the Canaries. Other nations rushed to get a piece of the action. In 1501, the Portuguese began to depopulate Labrador, carrying the now-extinct Beothuk Indians to Europe and Cape Verde. After the British set up beachheads on the Atlantic coast of North America, they encouraged coastal Indian tribes to capture inland tribes. The Pilgrims and Puritans sold the survivors of the Pequot War into slavery in Bermuda in 1637. Charleston, South Carolina, became a major port for exporting Native slaves. The French shipped virtually the entire Natchez nation in chains to the West Indies in 1731.

A particularly repellent aspect of the slave trade was sexual. On Haiti, sex slaves were one more privilege that

Slave ships packed Natives from the Bahamas so tightly that a third of them died during the trip. In the words of Las Casas, a boat could sail from the Bahamas to Haiti "without compass or chart, guiding itself solely by the trail of dead Indians who had been thrown from the ships." The Bahamas were left "totally unpeopled and destroyed."

---

69. De Cordoba letter in Williams, *Documents of West Indian History, vol. 1: 1492–1655*, 94.
70. "Genocide" may be too harsh. The Spanish profited from American Indian labor on Haiti. They didn't want to wipe out the Arawaks. Many died from diseases such as malaria, which the Spanish introduced unknowingly. Disease and forced famine are factors in other genocides, however. Russell Thornton deliberately makes the comparison in the title of his book *American Indian Holocaust and Survival* (Norman: U. of Oklahoma Press, 1990).
71. *Pathways* goes on to tell that "*Spanish* settlers on Hispaniola complained to the Spanish government of harsh and unfair treatment" by Columbus but never tells that *Indians* complained. Elsewhere, it does mention that other Spanish enslaved Indians, however.

This old print shows a coffle of newly enslaved Africans marching to the ocean to begin the long journey to the Americas. In 1493, Christopher Columbus brought sugarcane shoots with him to Haiti. They grew well, as did Europe's appetite for sugar. In all, about ten million Africans were shipped as slaves across the Atlantic. More than half were put to work on sugarcane plantations.

the Spaniards enjoyed. Columbus wrote to a friend in 1500, "A hundred castellanoes are as easily obtained for a woman as for a farm, and it is very general and there are plenty of dealers who go about looking for girls; those from nine to ten are now in demand."[72]

Enslaved Natives died. To replace the Haitians, the Spanish brought tens of thousands more Indians from the Bahamas. American Indian slavery then led to the massive slave trade moving the other way across the Atlantic, from Africa to the Americas. This trade also happened first on Haiti, started by Columbus's son in 1505. Predictably, Haiti then had the first large-scale slave revolt, blacks and Natives together. It began in 1519 and was finally resolved by the Spanish in the 1530s.

The Role of Columbus

Columbus introduced two processes of race relations that transformed the modern world: first, the taking of land, wealth, and labor from indigenous peoples, leading to

their extermination; and second, the transatlantic slave trade. As Sale poetically sums up, Columbus's "second voyage marks the first extended encounter of European and American Indian societies, the clash of cultures that was to echo down through five centuries." The seeds of that five-century conflict were sown in Haiti between 1493 and 1500. These are not mere details that our textbooks omit but basic information, crucial to understanding American and world history.[73]

Here is a direct implication for United States history. Captain John Smith used Columbus as a role model in proposing a get-tough policy for the Virginia Indians in 1624:

> The manner how to suppress them is so often related and approved, I omit it here: And you have twenty examples of the Spaniards how they got the West Indies, and forced the treacherous and rebellious infidels to do all manner of drudgery work and slavery for them, themselves living like soldiers upon the fruits of their labors.[74]

The methods unleashed by Columbus are, in fact, the larger part of his entire significance. After all, they worked. The Spanish so pacified Haiti that Spanish convicts, given a second chance on Haiti, could "go anywhere, take any woman or girl, take anything, and have the Indians carry him on their backs as if they were mules."[75] Citizens of other nations wanted the same ease. In 1499, when Columbus finally found significant amounts of gold on Haiti, Spain became the envy of Europe.

After 1500, Portugal, France, Holland, and Britain began to join Spain in conquering the Americas. These other nations were even more brutal than Spain. At least the Spanish made use of Native labor. As Columbus wrote, "The Indians of Hispaniola were and are its very wealth, because they are the ones who till the land, provide the bread and other victuals for the Christians, dig the mines for gold, and do all the work which men and beasts usually do." Some Spanish men even married Native women, too. The British didn't behave like that.[76] They simply forced the Indians out of the way. Natives sometimes fled to Spanish lands (Florida, Mexico) to get better treatment.

72. Letter by Columbus quoted in Williams, *Documents of West Indian History, vol. 1, 1492–1655*, 36–37. Las Casas quoted in Ronald Sanders, *Lost Tribes and Promised Lands: The Origins of American Racism* (Boston: Little, Brown, 1978), 131.
73. *Conquest of Paradise*, 129.
74. Quoted in Sanders, *Lost Tribes and Promised Lands*, 290.
75. Koning, *Columbus, His Enterprise*, 86, paraphrasing Ferdinand Columbus.
76. Yes, there were exceptions, such as John Rolfe, who married Pocahontas, but they were few.

TEXTBOOKS OMIT CHANGES THE AMERICAS CAUSED IN EUROPE AND AFRICA

Columbus's findings caused almost as much change in Europe as in the Americas. The first change was medical. Syphilis began to plague Spain and Italy shortly after the return of ships from Columbus's second voyage. The French, when they caught it, called syphilis the "Spanish disease." Then the Germans called it the "French disease," and so on. Related diseases existed in Africa and perhaps Europe, but syphilis probably came from America. On the other hand, more than 200 drugs come from American plants whose pharmacological uses were first discovered by American Indians.

The Americas Shook Europe Religiously

More far-reaching was the religious impact of the Americas. In 1492, Europe was under the grip of the Catholic Church. As *The Larousse Encyclopedia of Modern History* puts it, before America, "Europe was virtually incapable of self-criticism." Although the American lands enriched the most Catholic monarchy in Europe, they also shook Europe's religious uniformity. How were these new peoples to be explained? By no stretch of the imagination were they in the Bible. Moreover, unlike the Muslims, who might be written off as "damned infidels," Native Americans had not rejected Christianity; rather, they had never encountered it. Were they therefore doomed to hell? Some people tried to claim American Indians were "the lost tribes of Israel," but that didn't work. Americans simply didn't fit within orthodox Christianity's explanation of the moral universe.

The animals, too, posed a religious challenge. According to the Bible, at the dawn of creation, all animals lived in the Garden of Eden. Later two of each entered Noah's ark and ended up on Mt. Ararat. The Garden of Eden and Mt. Ararat were both in the Middle East, so where could these new American animals have come from? Perhaps the Bible didn't know everything. Such questions shook orthodox Catholic thinking and contributed to the Protestant Reformation, which began with Luther's 95 theses in 1517, 25 years after Columbus first landed. The new plants, animals, and peoples also prompted new developments in science.[77]

Ideas of Liberty and Equality

Examples of American Indian societies transformed European political thinking, too. Societies like the Arawaks—without monarchs, without much hierarchy—stunned Europeans. The first major new work in political philosophy was Thomas More's *Utopia*. More wrote it in 1516 and based it on early reports about the Incas' society in Peru. Other European political thinkers influenced by American Indian ideas include Rousseau, Montaigne, and Montesquieu, whose theories led to democracy, and, later on, Karl Marx and Friedrich Engels, whose theories led to communism.[78]

When British colonists reached America, the lack of governmental force in Native societies impressed them. "All their government is by Counsel of the Sages," said Benjamin Franklin. "There is no Force; there are no Prisons, no officers to compel Obedience, or inflict Punishment." When he was arguing for the colonies to unite,

As a symbol of the new United States, Americans used the eagle clutching thirteen arrows, which they knew to be the symbol of the Iroquois League. The Iroquois Confederacy united six American Indian nations under one leadership. It provided one model for our own national government. Iroquois noted that although one arrow is easily broken, no one can break six (or thirteen) at once. This is the Great Shield of the United States.

77. Crosby, *The Columbian Exchange*, 11–12. See also Angus Calder, *Revolutionary Empire* (New York: Dutton, 1981), 13–14; Marcel Dunan, ed., *Larousse Encyclopedia of Modern History* (New York: Crescent, 1987), 40; Crone, *Discovery of America*, 184.
78. Arthur Morgan, *Nowhere Was Somewhere* (Chapel Hill: U. of North Carolina Press, 1946); William Brandon, *New Worlds for Old* (Athens: Ohio U. Press, 1986).

well before the Revolutionary War, Franklin held up the Iroquois League as an example. Some Indian societies cohered and governed large areas, like the Iroquois, while not constricting the freedoms of their citizenry. Women also held more status and power in most Native American societies than in white societies of the time. African American slaves fled to American Indian societies whenever they could. For a hundred years after the Revolutionary War, Americans credited Natives as a source of our democratic institutions. Revolutionary-era cartoonists used American Indians to represent the colonies. When Americans took actions to protest unjust authority, like the Boston Tea Party, they chose to dress as American Indians.[79]

Of course, Dutch traditions of religious freedom played an important role in Plymouth as well as New York. So did British common law and the Magna Carta. Our democracy stems from several sources. Two new American history textbooks mention that Franklin invoked the Iroquois example while arguing that the colonies should confederate. Even they do not note, as does a photo caption in *Discovering American History*, that "Franklin's Albany Plan might have been inspired by the Iroquois League." The other eighteen books are silent as to *any* possible influence of Native Americans on our form of government. Perhaps their authors see liberty, like navigation, as the exclusive development of Western culture.[80]

Europeans Become Racist to Justify Their Actions

The Americas contributed to European thinking in still other ways. The mere knowledge of their existence intensified European consciousness: suddenly America became "opposite" to Europe in ways that even Africa had not. Before 1492 there was no "Europe"; people were Tuscans, French, or something else. Now Europeans began to see similarities among themselves, at least in contrast to Native Americans.

Racism arose as the handmaiden of the new enslavement of Africans and Americans. Slavery had long existed around the world. American Indians enslaved captives; so did Africans. In Europe, nation-states enslaved Slavs—who did not have nation-states—so frequently that the word "Slav" became the generic "slave." But the new slavery, started by the Portuguese in Africa and the Spanish in America, was different. The power imbalance was so great between the Europeans with their ships and guns and the natives in Africa and America that it encouraged Europeans not to think of their opponents as equal human beings. From da Gama's behavior in front of Kolkata, to the Spanish extermination of the Canary Islanders, to Columbus's war on the Haitians, to the British enslavement of the Pequots, we can draw a straight line. That line also connects the Belgians' cutting off the hands of workers in the Congo, the Germans' exterminating the Herreros of Namibia, the Holocaust of Jews and Rom people ("Gypsies"), and the French burning entire villages in Madagascar in 1947. The "other" has no rights, if the power imbalance is great enough.

The new enslavement of "the other" also differed in that it offered little chance for upward mobility. It was always possible for Slavs to learn the language and culture of the people who enslaved them. Thus, gradually they stopped being Slavic. Their children, too, would not be Slavic and might even have a free parent. They might also get traded back to their home community for POWs from the other side. Enslaved Africans in America, on the other hand, or American Indians in Spain, had little chance to escape, either geographically or socially. Increasingly Europeans came to see "slaves" as "other races," "other races" as slaves, and "race" as an important human characteristic. Increasingly they also saw themselves as "white," different from "blacks" or "Indians." Eventually, and unlike earlier slaveries, children of enslaved African Americans would be defined slaves forever and could never achieve upward mobility through intermarriage with the owning class.

The rationale for this differential treatment was racism. The new harsher slavery had to be justified. As Montesquieu, the French social philosopher who had

79. Jose Barreiro, ed., *Indian Roots of American Democracy* (Ithaca: Cornell U. American Indian Program, 1988), 40–43; Virgel Vogel, *This Country Was Ours* (New York: Harper and Row, 1972), 257–59; James Axtell, "The Indian in American History, the Colonial Period," in *The Impact of Indian History on the Teaching of United States History* (Chicago: Newberry Library, 1984), 23; Bruce E. Johansen, *Forgotten Founders: How the American Indian Helped Shape Democracy* (Harvard, MA: Harvard Common Press, 1982); and Bernard Sheehan, "The Ideology of the Revolution and the American Indian," in *The American Indian and the American Revolution*, ed. Francis Jennings (Chicago: Newberry Library, 1983), 12–23. Not all Native societies were egalitarian: the Natchez in Mississippi and the Aztecs in Mexico displayed rigid hierarchies. According to Sauer (*Spanish Main*), so did the Arawaks, but other sources disagree.
80. Before 1492, China, Turkey, and North Africa had more religious freedom than Europe. Marco Polo reported that of all the fabulous things he saw during his 27-year trip to "Cathay," none amazed him more than its freedom of worship: Jews, Christians, Muslims, and Buddhists worshiped freely and participated in civil society without handicap (Marc Ferro, *The Use and Abuse of History* [London: Routledge and Kegan Paul, 1984], 5). Turks and Moors also allowed freer worship than Europe. Jews, who flourished in Spain under the tolerant Moors, were driven out by the Spanish when they recaptured control in 1492.

such a profound influence on American democracy, ironically observed in 1748: "It is impossible for us to suppose these creatures to be men, because, allowing them to be men, a suspicion would follow that we ourselves are not Christian." Here Montesquieu is presaging social psychologist Leon Festinger's idea of cognitive dissonance—that people mold their ideas to rationalize their actions. Therefore increased racism was another result of Columbus's voyages, since Columbus began the transatlantic slave trade west to east, and his son began it east to west.

Columbus's own writings show cognitive dissonance. When Columbus was selling Queen Isabella on the wonders of the Americas, the Natives were "well built" and "of quick intelligence." "They have very good customs," he wrote, "and the king maintains a very marvelous state, of a style so orderly that it is a pleasure to see it, and they have good memories and they wish to see everything and ask what it is and for what it is used." Later, when Columbus was justifying his wars and enslavement of them, the Natives were "cruel" and "stupid," "a people warlike and numerous, whose customs and religion are very different from ours."

Regarding American Indians, Columbus started this process of cognitive dissonance, but he was hardly the last to rationalize mistreating them. George Washington provides another example. Like Columbus, he held positive views of American Indians early in his life. Later, after unleashing the Ohio War of 1790 upon Native Americans, he denounced them as "having nothing human except the shape." In 1845, William Gilmore Simms, the Southern novelist, summed up: "Our blinding prejudices . . . have been fostered as necessary to justify the reckless and unsparing hand with which we have smitten [the Indians] in their habitations and expelled them from their country."[81]

New Foods and Wealth from America Transformed Europe and the World

The Americas shook not only people's minds, but also African and Eurasian stomachs. Today, almost half of all major crops grown throughout the world come from the Americas. Adding corn to African diets caused the population to grow, which helped fuel the African slave trade to the Americas. Adding potatoes to European diets helped cause the population to grow there as well, which helped fuel the European immigration to the Americas. The new crops also played a key role in causing the northern countries—Britain, Germany, and finally Russia—to become dominant powers. This transformed the power base of Europe, moving it away from the Mediterranean.[82]

Exploiting the Americas transformed Europe. First, American treasure enriched Spain, leading to the Spanish "Golden Age" of the 1500s. Ferdinand Columbus ends his biography of his father, "From those provinces and kingdoms there come to Spain every year many ships laden with gold, silver, brazilwood, cochineal, sugar, pearls, and precious stones, and many other things of great value, on account of which Spain and her princes today are in a flourishing condition."

Next, through trade with Spain and through piracy, other European nations prospered. Some authors hold that these riches led to the rise of capitalism and eventually to the industrial revolution. American gold and silver fueled an inflation that eroded the wealth of all the non-European countries in the world. This undermined Islamic powers and helped Europe to dominate the earth. Africa suffered too. The trans-Saharan trade collapsed, because the Americas supplied more gold and silver than the Gold Coast ever could. As a result, African traders switched to exporting slaves.[83]

Before 1992, Textbooks Didn't Tell Any of This

These consequences, triggered by Columbus's first two voyages, transformed history. Astoundingly, only one book written before 1992 described these geopolitical implications of Columbus's encounter with the Americas.

I had expected to find at least a bland "contributions" theme—how much American Indians had "given" to our modern world. I thought texts would at least mention food. After all, what is threatening about crediting Natives for beans, corn, peanuts, peppers, potatoes, and tomatoes? After all, our regional cuisines—from New England pork and beans to New Orleans gumbo to Texas chili—often combine American Indian as well as European and African elements. But only four of the sixteen books published before 1992 even discussed American Indian foods.

81. Simms is quoted in Lee Clark Mitchell, *Witnesses to a Vanishing America* (Princeton, NJ: Princeton U. Press, 1981), 255. See also Virgel Vogel, *This Country Was Ours*, 286.
82. Crosby, *The Columbian Exchange*, 124 and ch. 5; William Langer, "American Foods and Europe's Population Growth, 1750–1850," *Journal of Social History* 8 (Winter 1975): 51–66; Jack Weatherford, *Indian Givers* (New York: Fawcett, 1988), 65–71.
83. Weatherford, *Indian Givers*.

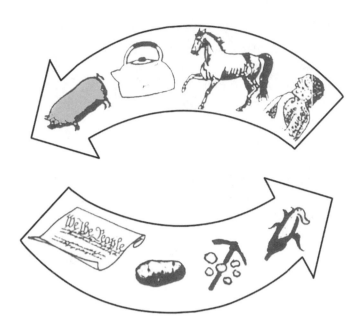

Products from each hemisphere transformed the other. Before 2000, most textbooks didn't mention any of this.

After 2000, five of the six new textbooks at last treated not only American foodstuffs, but also the diseases and livestock that went the other way. A couple also mention gold and silver, but not the impact of these new riches on the geopolitics of the world. *Pathways* notes that European laws and culture diffused from east to west, but no book mentions any impact of American Indian ideas from west to east.

Take a Position: What Were Consequences of Columbus?

Tell the key results of the European conquest of Haiti and the Americas. Why are these results still important today?

TEXTBOOKS MAKE COLUMBUS SEEM MORE TRAGIC

Although most authors can't find room for the impact of Columbus's voyages on Europe, they do tell what happened to Columbus. Unfortunately, most of what they say simply isn't true.

Having Columbus come to a tragic end—sick, poor, and ignorant of his great accomplishment—seems to make for a better story. "Columbus's discoveries were not immediately appreciated by the Spanish government,"

according to *The American Adventure*. "He died in neglect in 1506." The facts are just the opposite. "Columbus was honorably received by the king and queen, who caused him to sit in their presence, a token of great love and honor," reported Peter Martyr, the leading historian in Spain at the time. Ferdinand and Isabella immediately appreciated "Columbus's discoveries," which is why they immediately outfitted him for a much larger second voyage.

"[Columbus] was always trying to prove that he had found the treasure lands of the East," according to Boorstin and Kelley. "But he finally reaped only misfortune and disgrace." In reality, in 1499 Columbus made a major gold strike on Haiti. He and his successors then forced thousands of Natives to mine it for them.

"Despite increasing evidence that he had found a new continent," says *America, Pathways to the Present*, " . . . Columbus died a disappointed man, never knowing how much he had changed the course of history." Actually, Columbus reached South America on his third voyage and knew it to be a continent, as his own journal reveals. As he cruised the coast of Venezuela, he passed the Orinoco River. "I have come to believe that this is a mighty continent, which was hitherto unknown," he wrote. "I am greatly supported in this view by reason of this great river and by this sea which is fresh." He knew no mere island could sustain such a large flow of water.

Christopher Columbus died "poor, lonely, and broken-hearted," in the words of *Triumph of the American Nation*. Actually, he died a rich man in Valladolid, Spain, with relatives and friends at his side. His heirs were well endowed and spent much of the next three centuries suing Spain over just how much they would get.

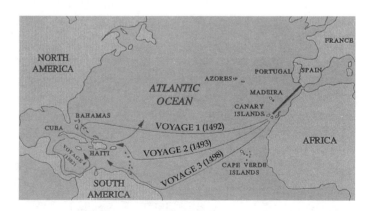

On Columbus's third voyage, he deliberately sailed farther south because Caribbean island Natives told him a continent lay south of them. On his fourth voyage, he looked for a strait through Panama to the ocean that Natives had told him lay on the other side.

This is Columbus's coat of arms, which Ferdinand and Isabella conferred upon him in 1493. It depicts the royal symbols of the lion of Léon and the castle of Castile, tangible proof of the high honors Columbus received from Spain. The other symbols represent sailing and the islands he reached. After his third voyage, when he sailed along the northern coast of South America, he had the lower islands merged to represent the continent. Owing to the curves in the design, it happens to form an accurate symbolic likeness.

WHY DO TEXTBOOKS LIE?

To ask why authors tell inaccurate history is to ask what is the purpose of American history courses and textbooks. A first answer might be simply this: so students know the history of their country. But that answer cannot explain why books leave out what Columbus did with the Americas, but include silly little details of his life that aren't even true.

A better reason might be that authors are happy being Eurocentric. All but one or two of the more than 50 authors credited with writing these books are whites whose families came originally from Europe. We noted that many Italian Americans, like Joe DiMaggio, identify strongly with Columbus. To a lesser degree, so do other Euro-Americans. Maybe the Columbus story that authors tell helps them to feel good about Columbus and consequently about themselves. Also, our society is more like Spain in 1492 than like Haiti. Therefore, it may be easier for authors to identify with Spaniards than with Arawaks.

Fear is another reason for leaving out details that might reflect badly on Columbus or, somehow, on the United States. Publishers want to sell books to the committees of teachers, parents, and school board members that choose textbooks. Publishers fear that if their book offends someone, s/he might argue against it at adoption time. Telling the truth about Columbus might offend teachers or parents who learned the old myths. Italian Americans might get angry. So might the Knights of Columbus, a large organization in the Catholic Church. It's safer to repeat what everyone else says, even though everyone else is wrong.

Another reason is laziness. Writing a history of the United States is a big job. It requires knowing something about archaeology and American Indian history, world history (especially of Europe and Africa), all the different periods (colonial, Civil War, Great Depression, etc.), women's history, the history of science and technology, race relations, and many other topics. Textbooks are supposed to be tertiary (third-level) works. Authors should base them on secondary sources—books and articles about each topic and time period, written by historians who evaluate the primary sources and combine them to tell a story. Unfortunately, textbooks seem mostly based on each other. Many authors take a short cut: they simply model their books after other books already on the market. Facts about Columbus—and everything else—get lost as authors get further and further from the primary sources and even the secondary sources.

One of the books I reviewed, *The American Adventure*, is mostly composed of maps, illustrations, and extracts from primary sources such as diaries and laws, woven together by narrative passages. Its section about Columbus includes several maps, the usual portrait, two pages of extracts from his journal, a letter, and excerpts from other sources. Even so, *Adventure* is caught up in the Columbus myth: its primary sources have been edited to omit anything bad about Columbus, so they present his acts even more favorably than Columbus himself did!

Sometimes the authors listed on a book's cover didn't even write it! Or sometimes they wrote only the first edition, decades earlier. Nevertheless, new editions come out year after year, written by unnamed assistants buried deep in tiny offices of giant publishing houses. In 2006, while reading the six new textbooks listed at the front of this book, I discovered an astounding case of plagiarism—passing off someone else's work as your own. For paragraph after paragraph, two books—*America: Pathways to the Present* and *A History of the United States* by Boorstin and Kelley—were almost identical. You might expect that this would lead to a major scandal in the history profession. It did prompt a front-page story in the *New*

York Times. After all, the level of cheating was far graver than merely using a quotation by someone else without quotation marks, which can get a historian in trouble. In these texts, the copying went on for page after page. Both authors chose the same photos; both used the same captions.[84]

It turns out that neither set of authors wrote the chapter in question. Indeed, none of the authors even *read* the chapter or *knew* who had written it. "They hired somebody," Brooks Mather Kelley told me. "I don't remember the man's name." No one seemed to care. Indeed, historians don't think much of other historians who *do* write textbooks, even when they actually write the books, rather than just renting their names to a publisher. "A successful textbook," wrote Thomas Bailey, author of *The American Pageant*, "would actually hurt me with some of my peers."[85] No major professional history journal reviews textbooks, even though they are read by millions of K–12 students across the nation. Therefore errors go uncorrected and plagiarism goes undetected for decades.

Textbooks Give Us "Feel-Good" History

Authors also lie on purpose. We know because they tell us their intention in writing their textbooks. The teachers' edition of *The American Way* states: "It is the goal of this book that its readers will understand America, be proud of its strengths, be pleased in its determination to improve, and welcome the opportunity to join as active citizens." That's very interesting. *Way's* author wants us to be proud of and pleased with America. It follows that she is hardly likely to pay reasonable attention to any bad things in U.S. history.

A History of the Republic tells students: "You will become familiar with the common experiences that bring Americans together as well as the diverse experiences that make American life rich and varied." Notice that *A History* doesn't mention events that have brought Americans into conflict with each other. Like *Way*, it emphasizes only positive "experiences."

A similar nationalist spirit runs through all of the 22 leading U.S. history textbooks that I examined. Even their titles are "rah-rah." Phrases like *The American Pageant*, *The American Way*, *Land of Promise*, and *Triumph of*

Doing History: Telling About Books from Their Covers

Examine the front cover of your U.S. history textbook. Is it nationalist? Compare its cover with those in other subjects.

the American Nation are not neutral. Rather, they inspire nationalism before the book is even opened. So do their covers, which sport eagles, the Statue of Liberty, and of course the flag. All six of the new books I examined, published since 2000, use red, white, and blue on their covers. These titles and covers are very different from other school books. Chemistry books, for instance, are usually just called *Chemistry* or *Principles of Chemistry*, not *Triumph of the Molecule*!

Thinking Well of Columbus Supposedly Promotes "Good Citizenship"

Textbook authors are trying to sell nationalism, a simple-minded form of patriotism. They believe this nationalism creates good citizens. Remember that *The American Way* is written so its readers will "welcome the opportunity to join as active citizens." How does Columbus fit in? Our textbooks treat Columbus as an origin myth: as Bill Bigelow sums up, he was good and so are "we." All the books discussed here want us to identify with Christopher Columbus—the one whom the State of Maine had in mind when it made Columbus Day a holiday in 1913. Maine's purpose was "to impress on the minds of the youth the important lessons of character and good citizenship to be learned from the lives of American leaders and heroes," the legislature said, so students could contemplate "their own duties and obligations to the community, state, and nation."[86]

When he set forth to get the United States to celebrate the Columbus Quincentenary, President George H. W. Bush stated his belief in this nationalist Columbus as hero and role model. Here is the lesson he wanted young people to learn from Columbus: "Christopher Columbus not only opened the door to a New World, but also set an example for us all by showing what monumental feats can be accomplished through perseverance and faith."[87]

84. In "The Ghost Behind the Classroom Door" (*Today's Education* [April 1978], 41–45), "Scriptor Pseudonymous" gives a behind-the-scenes account by someone who actually writes textbooks but never gets credit for them. Cf. Diana Schemo, "Schoolbooks Are Given F's in Originality," *New York Times*, July 13, 2006.
85. Thomas A. Bailey, *The American Pageant Revisited* (Stanford, CA: Hoover Institution Press, 1982), 180.
86. Quoted in Bessie L. Pierce, *Public Opinion and the Teaching of History in the United States* (New York: Knopf, 1926), 61–62.
87. Official statement, June 8, 1989, quoted in *Five Hundred* (magazine of the Columbus Quincentenary Jubilee Commission), October 1989, 9.

Authors selling this picture of Columbus add little details to help us identify with Columbus. They tell of his rejections before he finally got the money for his voyages. They show us how he thanked God when he reached land. And they invite us to feel sad for him, dying "poor, lonely, and broken-hearted," never knowing what he had accomplished. Authors who are pushing this Columbus have no interest in mentioning anything bad about him, so they leave out what he did with the Americas once he reached them—even though that's half of the story, and perhaps the more important half.

Thinking Well of Columbus Supposedly Holds the United States Together

Make no mistake: some people feel that teaching the truth about Columbus is un-American. Their slogan seems to be, a great country "deserves" a great founder. If Columbus wasn't so great, they get defensive: somehow our country might not be so great. A hundred years ago, some negative facts about Columbus surfaced when the United States was celebrating the 400th anniversary of Columbus's first voyage. Chauncey Depew, president of the New York Central Rail Road, blasted the critics as unpatriotic: "If there is anything which I detest more than another, it is that spirit of critical historical inquiry which doubts everything; that modern spirit which destroys all the illusions and all the heroes which have been the inspiration of patriotism." After the negative appraisal that Columbus got in 1992, philosopher Michael Berliner, writing for the Ayn Rand Institute, went even further: "The attacks on Columbus are ominous, because the actual target is Western civilization."[88] Similarly, Louis Rukeyser, the stock market analyst, claimed that people who criticize Columbus "are endangering this nation's ability to compete and flourish in the 21st century." How in the world could telling the truth about Columbus do that? It is divisive, Rukeyser argued. He even called it "paranoid."[89]

This is a scary line of thought. It says that in order for Americans to bond together as a strong nation, we must be lied to. Indeed, Berliner went on to claim that Native Americans are *better off* because of Columbus! His argument is on the left; the right column summarizes anthropological and historical thinking on the issues he raises.

Prior to 1492, what is now the United States was sparsely inhabited, unused, and undeveloped. The inhabitants were primarily hunter/gatherers, wandering across the land, living from hand to mouth and from day to day. There was virtually no change, no growth for thousands of years. With rare exception, life was nasty, brutish, and short: there was no wheel, no written language, no division of labor, little agriculture and scant permanent settlement; but there were endless, bloody wars. Whatever the problems it brought, the vilified Western culture also brought enormous, undreamed of benefits, without which most of today's Indians would be infinitely poorer or not even alive.[90]

We have seen that four million to twenty million people lived in the contiguous United States, about the population of Spain and France. Most farmed. Hunter/gatherers do not wander. Except in deserts and the Arctic, hunter/gatherers do not live from hand to mouth. Life expectancy at age one was probably about 70 years. American Indians had invented the wheel, but with no draft animals, they found it useful only for children's toys and calendars. All societies have at least some division of labor. Native societies often warred, but at their "edges." Rarely did they try to exterminate others. Violence skyrocketed after Europeans arrived, bringing guns and alliances.

Doing History: What Did Berliner Get Wrong?

Use solid historical and anthropological sources, primary and secondary, to evaluate the statements by Berliner (left) and Loewen (right).

Roland Libonati told perhaps the most outrageous lie about Columbus, when he introduced the bill that made Columbus Day a national holiday in 1963. "We owe to

88. Depew quoted in John Yewell, "The Day, the Pledge, the Myth," in *Confronting Columbus*, ed. John Yewell, et al. (Jefferson, NC: McFarland, 1992), 171. Michael S. Berliner, "Columbus Day: A Time to Celebrate," aynrand.org/site/News2?page=NewsArticle&id=6165&news_iv_ctrl=1021, 11/2002.
89. Louis Rukeyser, "Hold On to the Dream," *The Reporter Dispatch* (July 7, 1991).
90. Berliner, "Columbus Day."

this great emancipator and nobleman of the seas a signal national debt of gratitude," according to the congressman. "Emancipator" means someone who frees slaves. Historians have called Abraham Lincoln "the great emancipator." Here Congressman Libonati applied the term to the person who started the Atlantic slave trade![91]

The "Columbus Day" Approach to American History

The Columbus Day approach presents him as a hero and role model, no matter what he did. Textbooks and American history courses that follow this approach don't limit their lies to Christopher Columbus. If authors omit anything unpleasant about Columbus, who never even set foot on U.S. soil (except Puerto Rico), how do you think they will present George Washington, Woodrow Wilson, or Helen Keller? Surely they will all get the heroic treatment.

Our best teachers encourage thinking by getting students to go beyond their textbooks. But teachers are sometimes tempted to present our leaders as heroes and role models. Teachers can also feel they have to maintain their role as "givers of answers." Then when they get hit by a question that challenges Columbus's or America's goodness, they can feel threatened. It's easy for a teacher to feel his/her job is to teach the textbook, not question it. At least that way, they won't get in trouble with parents, the principal, or the board of education.

Eventually, the whole country gets the heroic treatment! As *Triumph of the American Nation* puts it: "[Students] also discover how a set of common beliefs has

---

Doing History: Patriotism versus Nationalism

Defining "the duty of a true patriot," Frederick Douglass wrote: "He is a lover of his country who rebukes and does not excuse its sins."[92] Nationalists, on the other hand, take pride in their country, right *or* wrong, and may deny that America ever *has* been wrong, at least not intentionally. Examine your U.S. history textbook. Can you find examples of nationalism? of patriotism?

---

united the American people—young and old, men and women, immigrants and minorities—for more than 200 years. Together these values and ideas form the basis of the American heritage." No problem! Or at least no real problems—just 200 (or 500) years of uninterrupted harmony and progress.

Other countries teach history this way, too. But when they do, we don't like it. Before the fall of communism, for instance, Russia taught only good stuff about Lenin and Stalin. We scoffed at their textbooks. Now we must learn to read our own more critically.

COLUMBUS AND THE "CENTURY OF PROGRESS"

Related to this feel-good nationalism is the story line of progress. Saturating U.S. history textbooks is the theme of the United States as the land of progress. Boorstin and Kelley, for example, begin with a rosy view of our progressive past: "American history is the story of a magic transformation," and then end on the same note: "Americans have been planters in this faraway land, builders of cities in the wilderness, Go-Getters. Americans—makers of something out of nothing—have delivered a new way of life to far corners of the world."

This theme of progress affects the way authors treat Columbus. If we take for granted that the United States is the most progressive society imaginable, then the man who "made it all possible" *must* be a hero, no matter what he did![93] If progress was the result, who cares about the deaths of a few Indians (actually, as we have seen, 3 million on Haiti alone, and perhaps 70 million in all the Americas)?

The Columbian Exchange Is a Dangerous Process

However, we cannot count on unending progress. In 1493 Columbus started the vast process we now call the Columbian Exchange. Crops, animals, ideas, and diseases began to cross the oceans regularly. Today the United States exports rice, an Asian crop. Argentina exports beef, a Eurasian animal. Szechuan cooking in China is

---

91. Hearings on "Declaring October 12 To Be a Legal Holiday (Columbus Day)," House of Representatives, Committee on the Judiciary, December 18, 1963, 6–7; also Congressional Record — House, 9/10/1963, 21878. mocavo.com/Congressional-Record-Volume-110-7/695872/72.

92. Widely quoted, including on the inside cover of Robert Moore, *Reconstruction: The Promise and Betrayal of Democracy* (New York: CIBC, 1983). Today Douglass, who was a leading feminist, would doubtless rephrase to include women, implicitly incorporated in "he."

93. In turn, since textbooks present the United States as the most progressive society imaginable, then they will tend to depict its founder George Washington and almost everyone else connected with it as heroes, too, no matter what they did.

spicy because of hot peppers domesticated by American Indians. Italian food depends upon the tomato, also from America. Rabbits from Europe overran Australia. Syphilis from America overran Eurasia.

It is too late to lament all this. Besides, some of it, like Szechuan food, is wonderful! But the process is also dangerous. Research in the last 25 years suggests that long-run progress may not have been the result of Columbus's journeys. Consider Haiti, now called Hispaniola. Columbus and the Spanish transformed the island biologically: they introduced diseases, plants, and livestock. The pigs, hunting dogs, cows, and horses multiplied endlessly, causing tremendous environmental damage. By 1550, "thousands upon thousands of pigs" in the Americas had all descended from eight that Columbus brought over in 1493. In 1518 a Spanish settler wrote to a friend in Spain, "although these islands had been, since God made the earth, prosperous and full of people lacking nothing they needed; yet . . . they were laid waste, inhabited only by wild animals and birds."[94] Later, sugarcane plantations replaced gardening in the name of quick profit. More recently, population pressure caused Haitians and Dominicans to farm the hillsides, which destroyed the topsoil. Today, the island is in far worse condition than when Columbus saw it.

Thus, we cannot use unending progress to rationalize misdeeds by Columbus or by ourselves. We need to investigate the impact of Columbus to learn how he changed the world for the worse as well as the better. If we only study the good stuff, then we condemn ourselves to be environmentally ignorant. Textbooks prompt us to accept our technology uncritically, because they simply assume unending progress. Las Casas said of Haiti, "It was the first to be destroyed and made into a desert." We must learn from Haiti's example. Then we can achieve a proper respect for our power to do harm as well as good on the earth.

Was God on Columbus's Side?

Our culture assumes not only that progress is on our side (and Columbus's), but also that God is on Columbus's side (and ours). Columbus thought so too. Of the destruction of Haiti, his son wrote, "The Lord wished to punish the Indians, and so visited them with such shortage of food and such a variety of plagues that he reduced their number by two thirds, that it might be made clear that such wonderful conquests proceeded from His su-

preme hand." The way our textbooks present Columbus fits right in with this assumption. Several older textbooks provide this detail, quoted here from *Triumph of the American Nation*: "On the morning of October 12, 1492, Columbus and his crews went ashore and thanked God for leading them safely across the sea." Other books tell how Columbus planted crosses everywhere, to claim

Most textbooks include a picture like *Columbus Landing in the Bahamas*. It is the first of eight huge paintings that dominate the rotunda in our nation's Capitol. John Vanderlyn painted it in 1847. Columbus seems to be thanking God, while others kneel or carry crosses. Illustrations like this show Columbus as a hero and invite us to identify with him.

Here is an illustration of Thorfinn and Gudrid Karlsefni giving thanks to God for landing safely on Vineland. No textbook shows anything like this picture, which might imply that God was on the side of the Norse when they crossed the Atlantic. And no text *ever* implies God might be on the side of the Natives.

94. Alfred W. Crosby, "Demographics and Ecology," typescript (1990), citing Las Casas. John and Jeanette Varner, *Dogs of the Conquest*, 19–20. Spanish letter quoted in Sale, *Conquest of Paradise*, 165.

the land for Christianity. Did God lead Columbus across the Atlantic? Pictures like *Columbus Landing in the Bahamas* and their captions imply that God was on Columbus's side.

Every November, when we give thanks to God for our nation's blessings, we imply that God is still on our side. Perhaps we almost equate progress and God. Surely it's hard to imagine that God is on one side, progress on the other. During the entire nineteenth century most Americans believed that God and progress were both on *our* side.

Our Textbooks' Columbus Story Comes from the 1800s

Between 1811 and 1890, the United States fought more than 50 wars against American Indians, gradually taking over all of their land except reservations. In the last ten years of the century, the United States went beyond its shores to take over Hawaii, the Philippines, Puerto Rico, and Cuba. The national point of view in the 1800s would now be called "colonialist" or "imperialist."

In such a century it was natural for many Americans to make a hero out of Christopher Columbus. Columbus was also an imperialist, conquering American Indian tribes in the name of Spain. "Pierce the Rocky Mountains and hew the highest crag into a statue of Columbus," cried Senator Thomas Hart Ben-

The nineteenth century was a time of Columbus adoration. This "cigar store" Columbus in the folk art collection of the Shelburne Museum probably dates from the early 1800s. It shows Columbus as hero. Washington Irving's 1828 uncritical biography of Columbus went through many editions during the rest of the century. The 1893 Columbian Exposition in Chicago closed the century with an extravaganza that cost as much as the Panama Canal. This glorification of Columbus, during a century in which the United States expanded westward, conquered the last of the American Indians, and proclaimed Manifest Destiny, was no accident.

ton in the 1850s, linking our westward movement with Columbus's.

As usual, we didn't want to think badly of ourselves, so we didn't see ourselves as invading homelands, conquering tribes, and packing Native Americans off to concentration camps. Instead we said that our culture represented progress, science, and a higher form of religion. Similarly, we lied to ourselves about Columbus. You know now that many of the Columbus details that textbooks include never happened, such as his dying impoverished. Others did happen, such as the lookout crying "tierra," but are not especially important. True or false, these details became part of the Columbus story in the 1800s, the century of Columbus worship.

HISTORIOGRAPHY: HOW HISTORY CHANGES, DEPENDING ON WHEN AND WHERE IT IS WRITTEN

When I was in high school, I believed you memorized history the way you memorized the times tables. After all, Columbus did discover America in 1492, didn't he? Doesn't $2 \times 2 = 4$?

Historians know that history isn't like arithmetic. To be sure, there is a bedrock of fact in history. What happened in 1492 did happen, but that is not history. History is what we *say* happened. What we say about 1492 changes as we change. *Historiography* is the study of why and how history changes.

Our History of Columbus Has Been Colonialist

In all the Americas, admiration for Christopher Columbus is most concentrated in the United States. From cities like Columbus, Ohio, and Columbia, South Carolina, to hamlets like Columbus, Nevada, we honor

Columbus with more place-names than any other figure in American history save George Washington.[95] Why do we admire him so much?

To answer that, we must consider, who are "we"? Columbus is no hero in Mexico, even though Mexico is much more Spanish in culture than the United States. Why not? Because Mexico is also much more *Indian* than the United States. Mexicans don't celebrate him because they see Columbus as white and colonialist. We do as well, which is why we *do* celebrate him—and why we leave out all the bad parts. Thus, cherishing Columbus is a characteristic of white colonial history, not American history.

Doing History: Columbus on the Landscape

Find the nearest commemoration of Columbus on the landscape: a statue, monument, or historical marker; the name of a city, town, or county; a park, school, or street; a geographical feature; or a commercial center or government building. What does the site say about Columbus? (Unlike a marker or monument, a school, city, or geographical feature named for Columbus may not say anything, but *people* said things about the man when they proposed the name.) Do research to assess this history. If needed, propose a corrective marker.

We certainly can't expect Native Americans to join in. As George P. Horse Capture wrote, "No sensible Indian person can celebrate the arrival of Columbus."[96] Our textbooks don't just teach about him; they celebrate him. Thus, they alienate nonwhites. No wonder some people of color in this country demand new textbooks: right from the start, our history books are biased.

Colonialism Is Ending—Our Colonialist History of Columbus Should End Too

In the words of historian Michael Wallace, the Columbus myth "allows us to accept the contemporary division of the world into developed and underdeveloped spheres as natural and given, rather than a historical product issuing from a process that began with Columbus's first voyage." Maybe cheerful Columbus stories suited the nineteenth century, the era of colonialism—but they don't fit today's postcolonial era.

For two hundred years after Columbus's voyages, historians didn't bury the Spanish misdeeds. Theodore de Bry's illustrations of Spanish cruelty became famous all over Europe a century after the events he portrayed. Here is the passage from Las Casas on which de Bry based this woodcut: "The Governor of the Island with 60 horses and 300 foot soldiers called to him about 300 of the leaders of the Indians. . . . Having by craft got them together in a straw Cottage, he caused them to be burnt alive together with the house. . . . As for Anacaona the Queen, . . . he caused her to hang herself." De Bry never saw Haiti. Nonetheless, his illustration, though fanciful, is faithful to Las Casas's text. Today, not one textbook includes a single illustration by de Bry of Spanish-Indian interaction. Instead, books include head-and-shoulder portraits of Columbus that have no historic value.

How are the textbooks colonialist? We have seen how they get us to root for Christopher Columbus by including nice humanizing details. Only a few of the books express any horror at his treatment of American Indians. All of them express exhilaration at the "discovery" of the "new world." Most include thrilling landing scenes, but no book illustrates his mistreatment of Natives.

Here are two stories written about Columbus and his reaching the Americas. The contrast between them shows us how our histories are still colonialist. The story on the left encourages us to identify with Columbus. The one on the right presents an Arawak view. It is part of a longer account, written shortly after the event, of an Arawak *cacique* (leader) who had fled from Haiti to Cuba.

No doubt you have already guessed that the fragment on the left comes from an American history textbook

95. Sale, *Conquest of Paradise*, 5.
96. "An American Indian Perspective," in *Seeds of Change*, ed. Herman J. Viola and Carolyn Margolis (Washington: Smithsonian Institution Press, 1991), 186–207.

A man riding a mule moved slowly down a dusty road in Spain. He wore an old and shabby cloak over his shoulders. Though his face seemed young, his red hair was already turning white. It was early in the year 1492 and Christopher Columbus was leaving Spain.

Twice the Spanish king and queen had refused his request for ships. He had wasted five years of his life trying to get their approval. Now he was going to France. Perhaps the French king would give him the ships he needed.

Columbus heard a clattering sound. He turned and looked up the road. A horse and rider came racing toward him. The rider handed him a message, and Columbus turned his mule around. The message was from the Spanish king and queen, ordering him to return. Columbus would get his ships.

Learning that Spaniards were coming, one day [the *cacique*] gathered all his people together to remind them of the persecutions which the Spanish had inflicted on the people of Hispaniola:

"Do you know why they persecute us?"

They replied: "They do it because they are cruel and bad."

"I will tell you why they do it," the *cacique* stated, "and it is this—because they have a lord whom they love very much, and I will show him to you."

He held up a small basket made from palms full of gold, and he said, "Here is their lord, whom they serve and adore. . . . To have this lord, they make us suffer, for him they persecute us, for him they have killed our parents, brothers, all our people. . . . Let us not hide this lord from the Christians in any place, for even if we should hide it in our intestines, they would get it out of us; therefore let us throw it in this river, under the water, and they will not know where it is."

Whereupon they threw the gold into the river.

(*American Adventures*). Most of it never happened.[97] It is merely one of the many legends that cling to the admiral like barnacles. Why did *Adventures* print it? Well, the incident is melodramatic. It creates a mild air of suspense, although we know everything will turn out all right in the end. Certainly it encourages the reader to identify with Columbus's enterprise. It makes Columbus the underdog, riding a mule, shabby of cloak. It puts us on his side. Lastly, it occupies considerable space, so students can feel they have learned something about him, even though they haven't.

The incident on the right did happen. It was written down by Las Casas, who apparently learned it from Arawaks on Cuba.[98] Unlike the mule story, the *cacique*'s story teaches important historical facts—that the Spanish sought gold, that they killed American Indians, that Indians fled and resisted. (Indeed, after futile attempts at armed resistance on Cuba, this *cacique* then fled "into the brambles." Weeks later, when the Spanish finally captured him, they burned him alive.) No history book includes the *cacique*'s story. If they did, it might make the Natives the underdogs and help us identify with *their* side.

These passages offer one more example of how our textbooks include and even invent unimportant details that humanize Columbus and cause us to identify with him. Meanwhile, they omit any story that might undermine the moral or technical superiority of Europeans. Excluding the passage on the right, including the passage on the left, excluding the true, including the false, amounts to colonialist history. This is the Columbus story that dominated U.S. history textbooks until about 2000.

Doing History: Compare Your Textbook

I suggest that many textbooks improved after about 2000. Surely your textbook was published after that date. Compile a checklist of the most important criticisms of textbooks' treatment of Columbus. How does your book fare?

The nations all around the globe that were "discovered," conquered, and colonized by European powers are now independent, at least politically. We no longer

97. Sale, *Conquest of Paradise*, 92, 238, 344; Madariaga, *Christopher Columbus*, 170–72.
98. See Williams, *Documents of West Indian History 1*, 17, 92–93.

dictate to them as master to native, so perhaps we should stop thinking of ourselves as superior, morally and technically. A new and more accurate history of Columbus will be a big help in doing so.

OBJECTIONS TO TEACHING THE TRUTH ABOUT COLUMBUS

I have spoken to hundreds of students, teachers, and historians about Christopher Columbus. As a result I have collected several objections to my suggestion that we should teach the truth about him. Let me share them with you and try to answer them.

"They're Only Children"

Some people feel that we should not load so much truth onto students, at least before they're eighteen or so. "Let children enjoy childhood," they say. They may be right. Some fifth graders or even twelfth graders who read this book or see the illustration of American Indians committing suicide might have nightmares about it. But lying to children is a slippery slope—once you've started sliding down it, how and when do you stop? Who decides what to teach in an American history course whose authors have somehow agreed not to teach the truth? Why should children believe what they learn in school, if it's full of distortions and lies?

Doing History: The Impact of History

After learning about some of the misdeeds and negative consequences of Columbus's voyages, do *you* feel bad? Should you have been shielded from this book? Should others?

"Feel-Bad History"

Another attack on the kind of history in this book is that it's too negative, just as textbooks are too positive. This is a valid criticism. To compensate for the textbooks, I have emphasized what they leave out. Teaching history more even-handedly does not leave us a history without heroes, however. Our heroes become more complex: in some ways Columbus should not be a role model. Perhaps Las Casas should.

Thus, "feel-bad history" is not the cure for "feel-good history." I don't mean to preach that Columbus was "bad." His conquest of Haiti can be seen as an amazing feat of courage and imagination. He was the first of many brave empire builders. But it can also be understood as a bloody atrocity. He left us a legacy of racism and slavery that endures to some extent even today.

Both views of Columbus are legitimate. Indeed, his importance in history owes precisely to his being both a heroic navigator *and* a distinguished plunderer. If he were only the former, he would merely rival Leif Eriksson. Columbus shows us both meanings of the word "exploit"—a remarkable deed and also a taking advantage of. Authors should present both sides. They should no more justify his total "rightness" by what they include than condemn him to total "wrongness."

It's Not Fair to Judge Columbus by Standards from Our Time

Some people claim that Columbus was just a creature of his time. They criticize me for applying today's standards to yesterday's events. In 1493 the world had not decided that slavery was wrong, for instance. We have seen that American Indians enslaved other Indians, Africans enslaved other Africans, and Europeans enslaved other Europeans. Why attack Columbus for doing what everyone else did?

Again, this criticism has some validity. I offer three replies. First, if we are to use Columbus as a role model, surely we should at least mention things he did that we would not now encourage people to imitate. Surely we should not hide these facts behind euphemisms like "not good at politics or business."

Second, the slavery that Columbus began was far worse than previous slavery. This wasn't because Columbus was far worse than previous enslavers. Rather, Europeans had more power, compared to the Indians they now enslaved. Slavery in Europe had been among Europeans. Usually it happened to captives after a "just war." The same was true for slavery among Natives in the Americas. Children of slaves were considered free. After Columbus, however, slavery led to racism. Now *all* American Indians, and soon all black Africans, were by definition considered inferior, hence suitable to be enslaved—as were their children, grandchildren, and so on.

Third, some people at the time opposed the slavery, land grabbing, and forced labor that Columbus started on Haiti. Of course, the Arawaks resisted. Many Spaniards also objected. Priests on Haiti preached against abusing the Natives. Listen to this Christmas Day sermon in 1511 by Antonio de Montesinos:

In order to make your sins against the Indians known to you, I have come into this pulpit. . . . Tell me, by what right or justice do you keep these Indians in such a cruel and horrible servitude? On what authority have you waged a detestable war against these people who dwelt quietly and peaceably on their own land?

We have seen how Queen Isabella sometimes opposed slavery. So did most advisers to the court. It is legitimate to hold Columbus responsible for his actions.

Most Histories Omit Las Casas, the First Historian of the Americas

Bartolomé de Las Casas was the most famous European champion of American Indian rights. If we can't criticize Columbus because he is "our hero," then we can't appreciate Las Casas. That's too bad, because he might be a different kind of role model. He began as a plantation owner. Then he switched sides, gave up his plantation, and became a priest. Las Casas became the first great historian of the Americas. He lived past 90 and spent more years in the Caribbean than any other European of the time who wrote about it. He was a fine historian. He relied on primary sources and helped preserve them. He used evidence and reasoning to argue with other historians. He was also a man of action who tried to put his ideas of justice for American Indians into operation on working plantations that paid their workers a fair share of what they produced.

When Columbus and other Spanish and Italian writers began to argue that Native Americans were inferior, Las Casas pointed out that they were thinking beings, just like anyone else: "All the peoples of the world are men, and there is only one definition of each and every man, and that is that he is rational."[99] When other historians tried to overlook or defend the American Indian slave trade, begun by Columbus, Las Casas said starkly: "What we committed in the Indies stands out among the most unpardonable offenses ever committed against God and mankind, and this trade as one of the most unjust, evil, and cruel among them." He helped cause Spain, unlike France or Britain, to enact laws against Indian slavery. Although those laws came too late to help the Arawaks and were often broken, they did help some Native Americans survive. Centuries after his death, Las Casas was still influencing history. Simón Bolívar used his writings to justify the revolutions between 1810 and 1830 that freed Latin America from Spanish domination.[100]

As a sociologist, if I found another sociologist who had been so important, you can bet I'd include him. Yet 12 of 22 history books don't mention Las Casas.

The books are improving on this score, however: three of six recent books do quote Las Casas effectively. Las Casas was followed by other men and women who argued for fair treatment of Native Americans—Roger Williams and Helen Hunt Jackson are just two examples. Most textbooks still underemphasize Williams's idealism toward American Indians. Most used to leave out Jackson entirely. They almost had to. Since they underplayed anything wrong the United States ever did, they had no reason to include the absorbing stories of Americans who challenged us to do right. Happily, all six recent textbooks include Jackson. Why? I suspect because she is a woman of uncommon importance, so in the interest of including more women, books now also supply an antiracist white person.

THE RESULT OF ALL THIS IS BORING HISTORY

When they leave out Las Casas, textbooks omit an interesting idealist with whom we all might identify. When

---

Doing History: What Do Adults Know and Think?

If some of the information about Columbus's treatment of American Indians in this poster book was new to you, see whether it is also new to your parent(s) or other adult friends.[101] Are they interested? Do they wish they had learned the truth about Columbus when they were in school? Or are they upset that you are learning "only the bad parts" now?

---

99. Note that when he wrote, peoples and "men" were synonyms. Las Casas was *not* trying to argue that people are all one sex or that women cannot reason.
100. Las Casas quoted in J.H. Elliott, *The Old World and the New* (Cambridge: Cambridge U. Press, 1970), 48; Las Casas, *History of the Indies*, 289; John Wilford, *The Mysterious History of Columbus* (New York: Knopf, 1991), 40. Las Casas is justly criticized for suggesting African slaves be brought in to replace Indian slaves. However, he recanted this proposal and concluded that "black slavery was as unjust as Indian slavery" (*History of the Indies*, 257).
101. Research shows that the revisionist literature coming out of 1992 has not reached many Americans, 85 percent of whom still hold "simple traditional" views of Columbus, according to social scientists Howard Schuman, Barry Schwartz, and Hanna D'Arcy, "Elite Revisionists and Popular Beliefs: Christopher Columbus, Hero or Villain?" *Public Opinion Quarterly* 69, no. 1 (Spring 2005): 10.

they leave out the Arawaks, they offend Native Americans. When they leave out the possibility of African and Phoenician predecessors to Columbus, they offend African Americans. When they are Eurocentric, when they glamorize explorers like de Soto just because they were white, textbooks offend all people of color. And when they present a pious heroic portrait of Columbus, leaving out the "bad parts," they bore everyone.

Beginning with Columbus, then, American history as taught in most middle and high schools has become offensive to some and boring to most. History seems to be a lot of facts to memorize, rather than issues to get involved in. Some wonderful teachers deviate from their textbooks and interest students in the issues. On average, however, across the United States, students consistently rank history their least favorite subject. They also consider it unimportant.[102]

Doing History: Comparing Textbooks

Some of the 22 books I reviewed were clearly better than others. Check out the treatment of Columbus in your U.S. history textbook. How does it compare to the 22 books discussed in this poster book? Does your book try to get students to identify with Columbus? Or is it less biased? Does it include the Arawak viewpoint? Compare two different textbooks—perhaps those used in high school and middle school, or in "advanced placement" and "slow" classes.

If your textbook left the American Indian point of view out of the Columbus story, think about what else it leaves out as you read the rest of it. The very next person it presents after Columbus is probably Ponce de Leon. De Leon "discovered" Florida in 1513, "while searching in vain for this fountain of youth," according to *Pathways to the Present*. Actually, he was seeking more Natives to send as slaves to Haiti's gold mines, but no textbook mentions that. De Leon had already participated in the Higüey massacre in eastern Haiti. There, Spaniards taunted the Taino men, women, and children they had captured, while cutting off their hands and feet; then they disemboweled them while they were still alive. Later, as governor of Puerto Rico, de Leon forced the Tainos to search the rivers for gold, grow food for the Spanish, and carry them and their provisions everywhere on their backs. Las Casas detested de Leon for his treatment of the Natives. Sadly, no textbook says anything about any of this. Instead, "de Leon named the mainland 'Florida,'" Boorstin and Kelley tell us, "either because of the flowers there or the fact that he arrived on or soon after Easter (Pascua Florida, or 'Flowering Easter'). Unfortunately, he never found the magic fountain." Such a lighthearted tale! Maybe middle and high school students aren't mature enough to trust with the truth. So let's just entertain them with the fountain myth.

Take a Position: Your State Should Rename Columbus Day

Columbus Day is not set in stone. Years ago, Hawaii renamed the holiday Discoverers' Day, by which they commemorate when Polynesians reached the islands. South Dakota renamed it Native American Day, as have some tribal governments. Some cities call it Indigenous Peoples' Day. At least two states simply don't celebrate it at all. Should your state rename Columbus Day? Why or why not? If you conclude it should, ask your local state legislator to sponsor a bill. Give him/her a convincing statement of your reasoning and evidence.

FURTHER READING AND AN INVITATION TO A DIALOGUE

This brings us to a final question: have this poster and book given you the truth about Columbus? Is there more than one truth about Columbus? Just as you cannot believe history textbooks without doing more research, you also need to check out the information in this book and poster. Here are ten important sources for further research, listed chronologically.[103]

---

102. Joan M. Shaughnessy and Thomas M. Haladyna summarize "Research on Student Attitudes Toward Social Studies," from 1949 to the 1980s in *Social Education 49* (November 1985): 692–95. They concluded, "Most students in the United States, at all grade levels, found social studies to be one of the least interesting, most irrelevant subjects in the school curriculum." See also Mark Schug et al., "Why Kids Don't Like Social Studies," *Social Education 48* (May 1984): 382–87. In a national poll taken by Widmeyer Research in 2009, high school students ranked social studies less important to their future career than ten other fields. See *Attitudes Toward Math and Science Education Among American Students and Parents: Summary of Findings*, opportunityequation.org/.../93d000e5-6a2b-44cf-8751-aec7a689587e?, 42.
103. Also you can check the sources in the footnotes throughout this book. Do they say what I say they say? What else do they teach about Columbus?

The Journal of Christopher Columbus (as summarized, paraphrased, and quoted by Bartolomé de Las Casas). There are many editions. An inexpensive translation is by Cecil Jane (New York: Bonanza Books, 1989) and includes a letter by Columbus written while homeward bound. Of course, this book treats only the 1492–93 voyage.

Bartolomé de Las Casas, *History of the Indies*, translated and edited by Andrée Collard (New York: Harper and Row, 1971). Las Casas's *History* runs three volumes; he also wrote several other books about the Spanish and the American Indians. We need a new one-volume summary, highly readable and focused. Until then, this book will have to do. Its first 145 pages cover Columbus and Haiti. The introduction by the translator is also important.

Alfred W. Crosby, *The Columbian Voyages, the Columbian Exchange, and Their Historians* (Washington, D.C.: American Historical Association, 1987). This booklet tells how the world changed as a result of Columbus's first two voyages.

William McNeill, *The Age of Gunpowder Empires, 1450–1800* (Washington, D.C.: American Historical Association, 1989). This booklet tells how and why Europe was able to subdue the Americas and the rest of the world.

Milton Meltzer, *Columbus and the World Around Him* (New York: Franklin Watts, 1990). Although written for junior and senior high school students, this book is not "dumbed down" and gives more than the usual heroic treatment of Columbus.

Lorenzo Camusso, *The Voyages of Columbus, 1492–1504* (New York: Dorset Press, 1991). Loaded with illustrations, yet inexpensive, this book is a good resource.

When Worlds Collide, Newsweek special issue (Fall 1991). This magazine offers readable compact treatments of many issues, from archaeology to Columbus's background to the sweeping worldwide changes caused by Native American crops and wealth. See also Herman J. Viola and Carolyn Margolis, eds., *Seeds of Change* (Washington: Smithsonian Institution Press, 1991).

Bill Bigelow, Barbara Miner, and Bob Peterson, eds., *Rethinking Columbus: The Next 500 Years* (Milwaukee: Rethinking Schools, 1998). Teachers and students will both enjoy these punchy articles. Some are primary sources from Columbus's time; others go all the way down to our time, including current issues facing Native Americans.

Howard Zinn, *A People's History of the United States* (New York: HarperCollins, 2001), chapter one. Zinn intended his textbook to be different from others. Beginning with his treatment of Columbus, it is!

James W. Loewen, *Teaching What Really Happened* (New York: Teachers College Press, 2010). Chapters 5 ("How and When Did People Get Here?") and 6 ("Why Did Europe Win?") relate to this book and suggest ways to teach these matters.

Doing History: Your Own Source

Discover an article, book, video, website, or other resource that relates to some part(s) of this poster book. Critique it, based on points drawn from this book and your own research. Recommend it to others, including me, if you think it's really good. Finally, if from your research you conclude that something I wrote here is wrong or misleading, please e-mail me: jloewen@uvm.edu.

INDEX

ILLUSTRATION CREDITS FOR BOOKLET AND POSTER

Grateful acknowledgment is made to the following for permission to reprint illustrations:
Catlin (page 2), *Tenochtitlan* (page 4)—Smithsonian Institution; *Adam Nordwall with Pope* (page 8)—courtesy of Adam Nordwall; *Olmec basalt head* (page 21)—Wikimedia Commons; *Semitic head* (page 22)—Alexander von Wunthenau; *Rotunda paintings* (pages 24 and 48), *T-shirt* (page 31), *Norse praying* (page 48)—Library of Congress; *Three ships* (page 33)—Robert Sachs; *Globe* (page 34)—American Geographical Society Collection, University of Wisconsin-Milwaukee Library; *Dogs attack Indians* (page 36), *Indians commit suicide* (page 37), *Burning hut* (page 50)—New York Public Library; *Wake* (page 38), *Slave coffle* (page 39)—Mansell Collection; *Map* (page 43)—Department of Geography, University of Vermont; *Coat of arms* (page 44)—Museo Navale di Pegli, Genoa; *Statue* (page 49)—Shelburne Museum, Shelburne, Vermont (photograph by Ken Burris); *Spaniard with pikes* (poster)—© National Geographic Society (painting by Arthur Shilstone); *Tenochtitlan* (poster)—Ignacio Marguina.